# Take Action

## FIGHTING FOR WOMEN & GIRLS

Stephenie Foster

# Take Action

## FIGHTING FOR WOMEN & GIRLS

Stephenie Foster

For inquiries, use the CONTACT page on the author's website:

# stepheniefoster.com

Publisher's Cataloging-In-Publication Data
(Prepared by The Donohue Group, Inc.)

Names: Foster, Stephenie, author. | Mikulski, Barbara, writer of supplementary textual content.
Title: Take action : fighting for women & girls / Stephenie Foster ; [foreword by U.S. Senator Barbara M. Mikulski].
Description: First edition. | [Washington, D.C.] : [Stephenie Foster], [2021]
Identifiers: ISBN 9780578876146 (hardcover)
Subjects: LCSH: Women's rights--Handbooks, manuals, etc. | Human rights advocacy--Handbooks, manuals, etc. | Sex discrimination--Prevention--Handbooks, manuals, etc. | Women political activists--Handbooks, manuals, etc.
Classification: LCC HQ1236 .F67 2021 | DDC 323.3/4--dc23


ISBN: 978-0-578-87614-6 (paperback)
ISBN: 978-1-647-04478-7 (hardcover)
ISBN: 978-1-647-04477-0 (eBook)
LCCN: 202 190 9689


Book design and production by Richard Whittington whittingtonandco.com
Edited and produced by Colleen Daly derbydog.biz


Printed in the U.S.A. or Canada by X?X?X?X?X?X

First Edition
10   9   8   7   6   5   4   3   2   1

# Acknowledgements

People often say, "It takes a village," and indeed it has taken one to get me to this point. I am thankful to the countless women and men across the globe who have inspired me and taught me many lessons throughout my career and travels. You are the reason I am committed to advancing gender equality and elevating women's voices.

It has been quite a journey for me, from being a litigation partner at a law firm to working on Capitol Hill and in the U.S. State Department, and everything in between. I started out with an interest in law and domestic policy issues – primarily around women's rights – and never envisioned myself working in the foreign policy and international affairs arena. But so many people along the way gave me opportunities, encouraged me, expanded my worldview, and guided me, and I am grateful to each of them.

There are so many people to thank, and in the interest of not excluding anyone, I will keep these acknowledgements short.

First, many thanks to the other co-founder of Smash Strategies, Susan Markham, who is a wonderful friend, business partner and collaborator, and great at challenging my thinking and analysis.

Second, thanks to the three people who have helped this book become a reality: Colleen Daly, an incredible editor; Lauren Supina, an innovative thinker on social media and public engagement; and, Denise Starr, who made sure I got the details right.

# About the Author

Stephenie Foster, a recognized voice in women's leadership and empowerment, is a partner and co-founder of Smash Strategies, a consulting firm that helps institutions achieve better results by focusing on women's leadership and gender equality. She has deep and broad expertise in women's economic and political empowerment, and decades of experience on Capitol Hill, in the Executive Branch, the nonprofit sector, and the law.

Foster served at the U.S. Department of State from 2012-2017, including as a Senior Advisor and Counselor to the Ambassador-at-Large for Global Women's Issues. She has represented the United States in numerous multilateral and bilateral forums, and also served at the U.S. Embassy in Kabul, Afghanistan, where she focused on women and civil society and traveled extensively throughout the country to work with individuals and organizations advancing the role of women in Afghan society.

Prior to joining the State Department, Foster served as Chief of Staff to two United States Senators (Barbara Mikulski (D-MD) and Christopher Dodd (D-CT)), and was appointed by President Clinton as General Counsel of the U. S. General Services Administration from 1999-2001.

A sought-after public speaker on topics including women's leadership, politics, women's role in peace and security, economic empowerment, and international women's rights, she has published multiple articles on women's global engagement in politics, the economy, and society.

Foster began her career as an attorney, and was a litigation partner in San Francisco, California.

For a more in-depth biography, visit Foster's website: StephenieFoster.com

# Contents

# Foreword

It was the spring 1966 when I first heard about a 16-lane interstate expressway slated to run right through the neighborhoods of East Baltimore, including Canton and Fells Point, Westside neighborhoods like Rosemont, Sharp-Leadenhall, and Leakin Park, as well as what we now call Inner Harbor. The plans to connect three interstate highways (95 to the east, 83 from the north, and 70 from the west) would uproot entire neighborhoods, displace many small businesses, and force thousands of families to move elsewhere. As a graduate of the University of Maryland School of Social Work with experience in community organizing, I was asked to attend a meeting to save these neighborhoods.

The first meeting was held in St. Stanislaw's Church Hall, where we decided we were ready to fight. We held neighborhood meetings that brought together both Black and White community members from East and West Baltimore to form coalitions based on mutual respect, mutual need, and mutual efforts. We led creative protests throughout the city, from organizing community festivals to show the value of our neighborhoods, to an organized education campaign featuring flyers, press releases, car signs, banners, and even a sound truck.

The night of the first meeting we formed SCAR – Southeast Committee Against the Road. And later at a community festival, I was quoted as saying, "The British couldn't take Fells Point, the termites couldn't take Fells Point, and the State Roads Commission can't take Fells Point."

Two years later I ran for and was elected to the Baltimore City Council where I continued the fight. Using all of the tools available to me as a Councilwoman, from legislation to zoning, and joining with the continued efforts of long-standing community groups with a shared commitment to our grassroots organizing strategy, we stopped the road – and along the way we built a stronger community.

From there, I got more involved in politics, running for the U.S. House, and then the U.S. Senate. While in Congress, I worked on issues for my community and the great state of Maryland. I also fought for women's rights: for the Lilly Ledbetter Fair Pay Act of 2009; for equal access to health care and prevention services for women, especially in the Affordable Care Act; and for retirement parity for homemakers.

With my deep roots in community activism, I will first say that I wish Stephenie's book had been around when I started my neighborhood Battle of the Road. In *Take Action: Fighting for Women & Girls*, Stephenie develops an advocacy framework and spells out how you, the reader, can implement the strategies and goals of that framework by understanding the objective you seek, mapping who has the power to make that change, asking key questions, and most importantly, organizing and taking action.

Her book is full of practical tools to help you effectively organize and advocate for changes that will positively affect the lives of women and girls here in the U.S. and around the world. Every day, despite their ambition and skills, women and girls face barriers to their full participation in the public life. You know that, and I know that. What's important is doing something, and organizing others to take action as well.

TAKE ACTION is focused around critical issues facing women and girls today:

- Access to education
- Economic opportunity
- Battling gender-based violence
- Political empowerment

You will be able to use the tools you learn here to turn protest into policy change and to take effective action in your daily life.

Stephenie served as my Chief of Staff and has become a friend. I have followed her advocacy efforts as she has worked to advance issues of women's leadership in the U.S. and overseas. Stephenie is committed to these issues at her core and has been doing this work since long before it became fashionable. She takes her experience and expertise, and the knowledge she carries around every day, and shares it in a readable, accessible way.

I thank her for doing this, and I thank you for committing to take action. We need all of you – your organizing skills and your energy – to create change. Each of us can make a difference, but together we can make change.

– **U.S. Senator Barbara A. Mikulski (D-MD)**

# Introduction
## Creating a Toolbox for Change

When I was a young girl, I asked my mother, a schoolteacher, why stories about doctors and lawyers all used the pronoun "he." What if the lawyer or doctor was a woman? I remember my mom saying that the pronoun "he" encompassed women and girls as well. Somehow that didn't seem right, but I didn't know why.

Over time, I came to understand why that bothered me. It meant that my life and my views were worth less than a boy's. Essentially, this has driven my work as a lawyer, activist, and advocate.

My work as an activist for policy change on behalf of women and girls – spanning over 30 countries and over 25 years – has led me to understand on a profound level that our world and its institutions are designed to value and benefit men while systematically excluding the voices of women. As government and private sector leaders – mostly men – struggle with fundamental issues including income inequality, climate change, the impact of pandemics, and racial injustice, they are unaware of or unwilling to acknowledge the disproportionate impact on women and girls, as well as the refusal of those who control institutions to give up power.

Make no mistake, despite continued challenges and global crises, there has been progress for women and girls in the last 50 years. Women have increased their participation in the global economy and we now hold more high-level corporate and management jobs than ever before. Women outnumber men in universities[1] and law schools[2] and are breaking barriers as politicians, CEOs, athletes, philanthropists, and scientists. Women, especially young women, are demanding fundamental change.

And, globally, **support for gender equality is strong**. In 34 countries surveyed by the Pew Research Center, 94% think it is important that women have the same rights as men, with 74% saying this is very important.[3]

Even so, women face significant barriers to their ability to fully participate in public and economic life, barriers that are based on social norms about what men and women "should" do. We now see these norms more clearly as we cope with, and respond to, the COVID-19 pandemic, where the gaps in caregiving responsibilities are highlighted, where women are on the front lines of healthcare delivery and retail services, and where there is an increase in gender-based violence.

Every day, despite their ambition and skills, women and girls in the U.S. and abroad face roadblocks that keep them from living the lives they want to live. Many women and girls experience these obstacles early in life, and as a consequence are subject to lifelong gaps in opportunity, income, and the ability to make life choices.

For example, because fewer women and girls study science, engineering, math, and computer science, there are fewer women in these jobs despite the equal capabilities of boys and girls in science and math. In many countries, girls are forced to marry while they should still be playing with dolls. Many women and girls are denied access to basic services, including healthcare and access to contraception. Across the globe, women and girls spend dramatically more time doing housework and caring for others than men and boys do. Millions of women don't have access to water, and must walk miles to collect water and/or firewood. Violence disproportionately affects women and girls. The majority of the world's poor are women and girls. At the current pace, it will take 145.5 years globally for women and men to achieve equal representation in political offices,[4] and at least 60 years for women in the U.S. to achieve the same.[5]

It's not unreasonable to become frustrated when you are confronted with these challenges in your daily life or when you read about them online or otherwise. It's easy to feel powerless to change things, to give up hope of ever making a difference. And yet, as noted above, there is ample evidence that women are effective agents of change, even if that change doesn't happen overnight.

I wrote *Take Action* as a guidebook, an instruction manual, a toolbox – for YOU. **I fiercely believe that if you, the reader, work by yourself or together with others as outlined in these pages, we can and will build on the progress that has been made, and we will ensure that opportunities continue to expand for women and girls.** Let's close our eyes for a moment and envision societies where women and girls have every opportunity, and then open our eyes and commit to taking action – big or small, for only today or every day, by ourselves or together with others.

The first step is to recognize and understand that the full participation of women and girls is critical to addressing the complex and daunting challenges the world faces today. In order to build stronger and more just societies and economies, it is essential to take into account the unique perspectives and life experiences of women and girls as policies and programs are developed across every sector in order to create prosperity and sustainability, equality, and dignity – for all.

We know, based on research, that increasing the participation of women and girls makes a difference.

- **When more women participate in the economy, families and communities and countries are more prosperous.** Gender equality and women's empowerment are powerful and effective tools that can generate tremendous resources for countries, both economic resources and social resources.

- **When women's participation in the labor force increases, incomes and gross domestic product (GDP) rise.** Changing the laws and norms that make it more difficult for women to participate fully in the economy has a real monetary benefit, not just for the women and their families, but for their communities and their countries.

- **When women are promoted to senior management and appointed to corporate boards, companies are more profitable.** Such companies invariably increase their bottom line. Societies with greater gender equality tend to grow faster and more equitably.

- **Economic growth and global security are intertwined**. Statistics show that the countries investing in women are more likely to be stable, democratic, and wealthy.

- **When more women participate in politics and public life, outcomes are more reflective of community needs.** Greater representation of women in legislatures has been linked to increased focus on health and family policy, environmental protection, and increased spending on social services.

- **When more women are at the peace table, peace lasts longer.** When women participate in peace processes, the resulting agreements are 35% more likely to last at least 15 years. Given that most peace agreements fail after five years, we cannot afford to ignore women's engagement as a powerful tool.

The next step in building on the progress that women and girls have made so far is to acknowledge that **women's empowerment and gender-equality issues are human-rights issues.** They affect the health and security of all families, communities, and countries. Including women is fundamental to increasing financial opportunities, strengthening democracy, and increasing respect for the rule of law – for everyone. There are some **important questions** to ask.

- Is it possible to highlight the laws, biases, and norms that consistently and effectively put women and girls at a disadvantage, and then **take concrete steps** to change those laws and adjust those social norms?

- **Can "normal" people help** create a world where every day, every person's voice can be heard, every person's safety protected, every person's talents engaged and appreciated, and every person's contributions compensated fairly?

The answer to these questions is a resounding **YES**. Over the course of my career, in both the domestic and international arenas, I have seen the difference that women and girls make in driving change, and the impacts that they have made.

I have witnessed firsthand that it is not only possible but absolutely necessary for people to participate in **individual and collective advocacy, action, and organizing**. For example, pressure from investors and consumers has caused some companies to change their business and hiring practices and to commit to producing goods free from child labor and human trafficking. Courageous women who tell their stories have instigated a sea change in our conversations about sexual harassment and assault. A record number of women have run for and won seats in the U.S. Congress and transformed the way we now envision who is eligible and capable to lead. Women political leaders from across the globe took decisive and effective action to address the COVID-19 pandemic.

*Take Action, Fighting for Women and Girls:*
- Provides a **framework for advocacy and action**
- Outlines **actions you can take in your daily life**
- Highlights **salient and critical facts**
- Spotlights **role models**
- Provides topic-specific **resource lists**

Overall, the book provides you with a **roadmap to address the persistent and systemic issues that keep women – and the societies they live in – from realizing their full potential**. It doesn't address every barrier or challenge, but is a framework you can use to work on any issue. *Take Action* is a **tool you can use** to play your part in this change and encourage others to do the same.

A group of entrepreneurs focused on women's leadership visit the U.S. to participate in the International Visitor Leadership Program sponsored by the U.S. Department of State.

The chapters in this book provide this roadmap.

- **Chapter 1** describes the critical role we all can play as advocates and activists for gender equality and women's empowerment, and underscores the importance of **advocacy** and organizing others to make change.

- **Chapter 2** discusses the power of **education** for girls and young women, the importance of keeping girls in school and making sure they can study what they want, and the impact of educated women and girls both globally and individually.

- **Chapter 3** discusses how to expand women's **economic opportunity** so that women can better support their families, so that communities can prosper, and so that economies can grow.

- **Chapter 4** discusses how to **eliminate gender-based violence** (GBV) and other harmful practices that make it difficult for women and girls to fully participate in society.

- **Chapter 5** discusses how to promote women's **participation in politics** and public life so that the policy-making process is more inclusive and current and future laws make sense for everyone.

In chapters 2 to 5, you will come away with the following tangible information:

- **Important facts** about each of the four main issues (education, economic opportunity, gender-based violence, political participation), and why each topic is **critical to the empowerment of women and girls**.

- **A framework for advocacy and action** that outlines specific steps and concrete actions you can take to help make a difference, including suggestions about how to take action in your daily life.
- **A Diving Deep** section that outlines what else you can do, and describes what **lessons we've learned** about what types of projects, programs, and interventions work, and which don't.
- Information about **role models**, women and men who are tackling these issues and acting as examples for all of us.
- A **Resources** section with lists of **movies, books, organizations, and links to facts and figures** that will inspire you as well as prepare you to be well informed about each of the four main issues. This information will be available and updated on my website: stepheniefoster.com

In each chapter there are **questions you can ask** – of political leaders, government officials, teachers, media executives, and others – to help start and drive conversations about what is possible and what actions can be taken to advance gender equality.

It is my hope that this book inspires you to act, sparks many conversations, and leads to concrete and sustainable change. We are all in this together. We can't afford to leave over half of our world's population on the sidelines. **Our future depends on it**.

## NOTES

1  Bilton, Isabelle, "Women are Outnumbering Men at a Record High in Universities Worldwide," Study International, March 7, 2018, https://bit.ly/3m3YkEC

2  Enjuris, "Where Do Women Go to Law School? Here are the 2018 Numbers," Before the Bar Blog, American Bar Association, February 28, 2019, http://bit.ly/WomenLawSchool.

3  Horowitz, Juliana Menasce and Fetterolf, Janell, "Worldwide Optimism About Future of Gender Equality, Even as Many See Advantages for Men," Pew Research Center, April 30, 2020,  http://bit.ly/OptimismGenderEquality.

4  The World Economic Forum, "The Global Gender Gap Report 2021," World Economic Forum, 2021, http://bit.ly/globalGenderGap.

5  Peçanha, Sergio, "What will it take to achieve gender equality in American politics?" *The Washington Post*, August 21, 2020, https://bit.ly/60YearsUntil.

CHAPTER ONE

# What Can I Do?

*If you don't have a good case and you don't have a good message,
then shining a light on it is not going to get you very far.*
Amal Clooney

*If they don't give you a seat at the table, bring a folding chair.*
U.S. Representative Shirley Chisholm

Social change happens because people like you and your friends take action.

As you know, women and girls face a combination of legal barriers, social and gender norms, lack of access to political power, and lack of economic and social resources. The challenges can seem overwhelming, frustrating, and at times enraging. But you can do something about it. You can decide to make a difference.

This chapter outlines concrete actions that you can take to jumpstart your own action plan for effectively advocating for women and girls, and will help you use the power of connection and organizing to make an impact. It will give you tools to start conversations and campaigns about the need for change and the need to be engaged.

What you do adds to what millions of others do every day, in ways large and small, to advance the status of women and girls. This includes:

- Advocating for new laws and repealing outdated ones
- Helping to make programs and services more responsive to the needs of women and girls
- Working to ensure that women have the tools they need to succeed at work and that they are able to work in a safe environment
- Fighting for girls' ability to study what they want
- Organizing your neighbors to address an issue in your community
- Raising your voice at work and in your community when you see a practice that impedes women's progress or is unfair

## LANGUAGE MATTERS

The word **SEX** refers to the biological differences that define people as male, female, or intersex (basically, the anatomy of an individual's reproductive system, and secondary sex characteristics). The word **GENDER** refers to the array of socially constructed roles, personality traits, attitudes, behavior, and values, and the relative power and influence that society ascribes to a person based on their biological sex. Gender is so embedded in our lives, our actions, and our beliefs that, unless questioned, gender roles seem completely natural.

More and more individuals identify as transgender or gender-non-conforming. **Non-binary** is an umbrella term for gender identities that are neither male nor female. **Cisgender** describes a person whose internal gender identity aligns with the sex assigned at birth. **Transgender** describes someone whose internal gender identity differs from the sex assigned at birth. Using **pronouns** that people request is respectful. In this book, I have noted where individuals use *they/them*. Otherwise, the people discussed use "traditional" pronouns.

This work takes place on every continent, in every community, and in every sector. It happens in big cities and small towns, on farms and in skyscrapers, in houses of parliament and in state houses, in corporate offices and on the production line, in schools and at home.

In this challenging time, it is easy to forget that each and every action we take can contribute to fundamental social change. In the United States, for example, while the struggle for civil rights and women's rights is ongoing and unfinished, tremendous progress has been made over the last 60 years, including laws that address outright race and sex discrimination in a person's ability to: vote, run for office, buy a house, obtain a loan, get credit, go to school, and apply for a job.

This progress, while uneven and not enough, happened because people across the country challenged the system in visible and not-so-visible ways. **Fannie Lou Hamer** was a civil rights activist in Mississippi who encouraged thousands of Blacks to register to vote. **John Lewis** marched across the Edmund Pettus bridge in Selma, Alabama. Four young Black men sat at a lunch counter in Greensboro, North Carolina. **Shirley Chisholm, Barack Obama**, and **Hillary Clinton** ran for President. **Sarah Palin** ran for Vice President. In 2018, **Alexandria Ocasio-Cortez** and **Ayanna Pressley** successfully ran against incumbent members of Congress in primary elections, shaking up the political system. In 2020, **Cori Bush** did the same.

In 2020, a record-breaking six women – **Congresswoman Tulsi Gabbard, Senator Kirsten Gillibrand, Senator Kamala Harris, Senator Amy Klobuchar, Senator Elizabeth Warren**, and **Marianne Williamson** – ran for President of the United States. On November 3, 2020, **Senator Kamala Harris** was elected Vice President of the United States. She is the first woman, the first Black person, and the first Asian-American to serve as Vice President.

In 1970, forty-six women sued *Newsweek* for sex discrimination and equal pay. Women asked why they couldn't get loans and credit cards in their own name.

The six women who ran for the Democratic nomination for President in 2020. Clockwise from top left: Congresswoman Tulsi Gabbard, Senator Kirsten Gillibrand, Senator Elizabeth Warren, Marianne Williamson, Senator (now Vice President) Kamala Harris, and Senator Amy Klobuchar.

Thousands attended protest marches, volunteered for political campaigns, or boycotted products in support of civil rights and women's rights. Women applied to military academies and "non-traditional" jobs. Girls fought to play soccer, baseball, and every other sport.

## FUNDAMENTAL PRINCIPLES OF ADVOCACY AND ORGANIZING

When you take an action on your behalf or for others, you are an advocate. Advocacy is a combination of vision, mission, and purpose. It's about planning and then acting to advance an idea and ensure that people's voices are heard by decision-makers and those who have power.

**Advocacy** can take many forms, use many approaches, and be informed by many strategies. Your advocacy and organizing can happen online or in person. It can encompass a variety of individual actions, including:

- Writing letters and sending emails
- Asking a question
- Making phone calls
- Instigating legal challenges to laws and policies
- Engaging in social media campaigns, including tweeting
- Donating money
- Lobbying for the passage or reform of laws or policies
- Organizing your neighbors or co-workers
- Participating in street protests
- Making a statement about something that you see as unfair or discriminatory
- Taking action in your everyday life

Activist Greta Thunberg striking for climate justice.

# INTERSECTIONALITY

The term **intersectionality** reflects the idea that gender, race, sexuality, disability, and social class not only shape how different individuals and groups experience life, but create interrelated systems of discrimination or disadvantage. Intersectionality encompasses the idea that people's identities are multifaceted and not just defined by one aspect of that identity, such as sex, race, ethnicity, or age. Few people would disagree that women of color face different challenges than White women, or that young lesbians face different issues than older Asian women. The concept of intersectionality helps us understand these dynamic and complex power relations in a way that is sensitive to differences both within and among groups.

**Kimberlé Crenshaw,** a law professor at UCLA and Columbia Law Schools, is credited with developing this concept. While conducting research about how to effectively address violence against women, she saw that policies developed by domestic violence shelters assumed that all women's life experiences are the same, when in fact they are not. As a result of that assumption, the shelters' strategies were not equally effective for women of color, who face different obstacles and challenges than White women.[1] Without this type of intersectional analysis, policies and programs miss the mark for large numbers of women.

**Here's a current example:** As we examine the impact of the COVID pandemic, the multiple layers of discrimination become clear. As of December 2020, 6.3% of women over 20 were unemployed, but those numbers were 8.4% for Black women, 9.1% for Latina women, and 11.4% for disabled women. At the same time, the unemployment rate for White men was 5.8%.[2]

Each of these actions make a difference and, when you organize and act in combination with other individuals or groups, they propel change.

One of the most compelling examples of individual action mobilizing others is Swedish teenager **Greta Thunberg,** who has become the face of the youth climate movement. Thunberg started small in August 2018, sitting by herself outside the Swedish Parliament every Friday to protest inaction on climate change. As she reflected on her decision, she said, "I was so frustrated that nothing was being done about the climate crisis, and I felt like I had to do something, anything."[3] Her hand-lettered sign said simply, "School Strike for Climate." In September 2019, just over one year later, 4 million people joined a global climate strike, the largest climate strike in history.[4]

The reason to take action is twofold. First, we all have the right to express our views and try to change policies with which we disagree. Second, decision-makers and those who work for them are responsible for genuinely considering everyone's views. It is important that policymakers hear from you about how women and girls are affected by laws and regulations on every topic from the design of transit systems to research on new medical interventions, to the development of new products and services.

We have seen time and time again that unless the views and experiences of women and girls are fully considered, laws and policies are incomplete and ineffective. For example, until pushed by a bipartisan group of women Members of Congress, the U.S. National Institutes of Health (NIH) conducted clinical trials of drugs only on men.[5]

In 1990, **U.S. Senator Barbara A. Mikulski** (D-MD) was outraged to learn that the NIH was ignoring its own guidelines and not including women and people of color in clinical studies.[4] Testing treatments on women, men, and people of different racial and ethnic backgrounds is important because there can be devastating health outcomes if doctors don't understand how treatments affect different people. **Senator Mikulski, Senator Olympia Snowe** (R-ME), **Representative Constance Morella** (R-MD), and **Representative Patricia Schroeder** (D-CO) led an effort compelling NIH to include women in their clinical studies.

Based on this research, we now know that:

- Nicotine replacement therapy is more effective in male smokers[7]
- Ibuprofen is a more effective painkiller for men[8]
- Women and men metabolize drugs differently[9]
- Men and women have different heart attack symptoms[10]

Testing only White male subjects misses these critical differences, and that can be fatal.

Traditional gender norms have granted men primary authority and responsibility over the public sphere because men are seen as leaders and responsible for working in the outside "dirty world" of politics and business.[11] On the other hand, women are traditionally responsible for the private (domestic) sphere, which includes raising children and responsibility for the household.[12]

Because we all "agree" that this is "normal," boys have been socialized to be active, to lead, and to speak their minds. Girls are socialized to be polite, to be good listeners, and to be consensus builders. These gender norms reinforce the idea that men deserve and in fact are endowed with power, and that women do not have power unless they somehow "earn" it or are explicitly given permission to wield it. Norms about who "naturally" exercises power and position underlie many of the traditional views we have of men and women and their place in society, and also inform ongoing policy debates about pay, pregnancy and parenting discrimination, sexual violence, access to health care, and access to education.

## ADVOCACY MAKES A DIFFERENCE

**Bellen Woodard** was an advocate the day she decided that not every "skin color" crayon was peach colored. As she said, when asked for the skin-colored crayon, the default was to pick the peach crayon. "I just want to ask [my classmates] what color they want because it could be any number of beautiful colors." Because of that simple question, everyone in her school started talking about skin color, and Bellen started *More Than Peach*, a project supported by Crayola, to send kits of art supplies and multicultural crayons to schools.[13]

**Malone Mukwende,** a 20-year-old medical student in London, noticed a lack of teaching about how certain symptoms appear differently on darker skin. In class he found himself repeatedly asking the question: "But what will it look like on darker skin?" As a result, he co-wrote a book for medical schools worldwide, *Mind the Gap: A Handbook of Clinical Signs in Black and Brown Skin* to ensure that patients with darker skin get better care.[14]

## Information is Power, and It Is Powerful

Information helps us understand the world around us. Gathering information about a situation or issue at your workplace, your school, your child's school, where you buy your groceries or daily coffee, or where you get your news, is critically important. Information helps to identify what change is needed, which is the first step toward advocacy on an issue. It's worth noting that sometimes advocacy focuses on protecting laws and policies already in place, such as a good policy on sexual harassment, or laws allowing access to family planning services.

Nearing retirement, Lilly Ledbetter, (2nd from left) discovered that she was being paid significantly less than her male counterparts, and had been for many years. Starting in 1998, she fought a complicated legal battle that she lost when the U.S. Supreme Court ruled for her longtime employer, Goodyear Tire & Rubber. However, her advocacy continued. In 2009, the U.S. Congress passed the Lilly Ledbetter Fair Pay Act, the first bill signed into law by President Barack Obama.[15]

Simple questions can help you gather critical information, and can also spark conversations fundamental to advancing the equality and empowerment of women and girls. Even if we don't have a lot of time to devote to activism, each and every one of us can ask one or two questions about the policies and practices of a business, a school, or any type of organization. These questions can happen face-to-face (even socially distanced), by email, by letter, by social media postings, or by phone.

## Simple Questions

Throughout *Take Action: Fighting for Women & Girls* there are lists of questions that you can ask across institutions – questions that are tailored for political and business leaders, financial advisors, teachers and school administrators, law enforcement, media executives, and decision-makers at your own place of employment. Use these questions, modify them, or ask other questions that work for you.

Asking questions can empower you. It also empowers those *inside* institutions who are advocating for change from within, thus provoking additional conversations about the issue you have raised. The more people ask questions, both from inside and outside of an organization, the more a company, a radio station, a law

Tarana Burke, the woman who helped us understand the widespread nature of sexual abuse and assault by using the phrase MeToo.

firm, a non-profit, a local or city or state or federal agency, or a service provider is under pressure to consider what it is doing to address the issues you raise. But first, you must define the change you seek.

## ADVOCACY AND ACTION: A FRAMEWORK

### 1. Identify An Issue You Care About

In order to ask questions that matter – as a first step in advocating for the empowerment of women and girls – decide what matters to you and what you want to see changed NOW. The most effective advocates are those who are working on something they are passionate about changing. For example,

- **Climate change** is all around us. We know that it disproportionately affects women and children across the globe, and that action to address climate change can take many forms.[16] As highlighted above, **Greta Thunberg** is a passionate and committed advocate and organizer on these issues.
- **Discrimination against, and unequal treatment of, women** in terms of access to education, jobs, and equal pay has an impact not just in terms of a woman's life *today* but also has long-term effects on her ability to support herself and her family, and save for the future.
- **Sexual assault and sexual harassment** are unacceptable and have tremendous negative impacts. This can occur at home, at work, at school, or on the street, and needs to be addressed in terms of changing laws and changing behaviors. In 2006, **Tarana Burke** began using the phrase "Me Too" to raise awareness of

the pervasiveness of sexual abuse and assault in society. This developed into a broader movement in 2017 when women started using the hashtag #MeToo following the Harvey Weinstein sexual abuse allegations.

## 2. Research: Do Current Laws or Programs Disadvantage Women and Girls?

Often, policies or programs that appear to be gender-neutral have a differential impact on women or other groups. For example, if the government office responsible for issuing business licenses requires online applications, that office assumes everyone has a computer and/or easy access to the internet. In many countries and in certain communities in the U.S., women are less likely to have computer and internet access, so an online process isn't gender-neutral, and can be a barrier to women's equal ability to file for a business license,[17] or to kids trying to do their schoolwork, as we have seen during the COVID-19 pandemic.[18]

In the U.S., women and men overall have roughly the same internet access, but poorer Americans, those with less education, Blacks, and Hispanics all have less access.[19] Across the developing world, nearly 25% fewer women than men have internet access. This data highlights how a process that seems gender neutral is not.

## 3. Investigate the Context So You Can Understand the Landscape

Make sure to understand how the issue you are raising plays out in a specific community, or in a specific economic sector, or company. There is rarely a one-size-fits-all solution to a problem. For example, girls can be dropping out of secondary school at the same high rates in two different communities. In one community the lack of women secondary-school teachers is the predominant reason because parents prefer a woman teacher as their daughters enter adolescence. But in another community the dropout rate is driven by the lack of safe restrooms in the school. Learning about how each community defines its needs and challenges is critical in order to advocate for solutions that make sense.

## 4. Find Out Who Has the Power to Make Change

Advocacy targets decision-makers. If you want to have an impact on governmental actions or policy, understand that the decision-makers are the government officials. They can include elected members of a legislative body (members of the U.S. Congress, a state or provincial legislature, a city council, or a school board or other elected body), and/or those elected and appointed in the executive branch (Presidents or Prime Ministers, governors, mayors, or heads of government agencies).

If you want to change corporate policy or challenge corporate actions, understand that the decision-makers are the CEOs, other senior executives, members of the corporation's board, and the shareholders. But there are many other types of policies and policymakers, including leaders of non-governmental organizations and foundations, members of the media, teachers, university administrators and professors.

After you have the basic information you need, the next step is to create a power map. This map helps you understand which organizations and individuals in those organizations have the power to make the change you seek or have relevant pieces of information. Your advocacy goal will dictate who you target with your questions. If you are trying to change a corporate policy about sexual harassment at the workplace, you will target business leaders or financial advisors. If you are addressing sexual assault on campus, your targets are educators, non-governmental organiza-

# THE POWER OF MAPPING

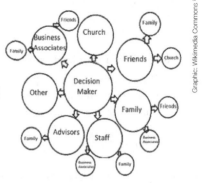

**Creating and using a power map** can help you understand who can (and does) influence a decision-maker, and can highlight any connections you might already have to these spheres of influence.

## Power Map Example

Your daughter and son both attend a local university. You are concerned about its policy on campus sexual assault, and you want that policy to be changed so that reporting is easier; perpetrators are subject to serious punishment; and survivors are treated fairly, receive support services, and are not stigmatized. In this situation the primary decision-makers on your POWER MAP are university administrators, the board of trustees, alumni, and professors. It is also important to engage with local and campus law enforcement, student leaders, and women's groups on campus.

tions (NGOs), and the media.

## 5. Define Your Interest in This Issue

Once you have identified your issue, and know who has the power to make the necessary changes, it is important to communicate to the person you will be talking to about why this issue is important enough to trigger your actions. Letting people know who you are and how you came to care about this issue does not have to be long or complicated, and in fact will be most effective when it is clear, concise/short, concrete/understandable, and convincing.

It is easy to fall into statements such as "I am for women's rights" or "I am for equal opportunity," but generalities don't give others a concrete sense of what you care about, nor do they indicate that you have taken time to think through your goals and your ideas about what needs to happen to make change. Instead of broad generalities, talk about the specifics of what you see as the issue.

## 6. Prepare Your Questions

Using the example of policies around sexual assault on campus, some questions should be focused entirely on information gathering, while others should be action-oriented.

### For the university administration, ask:

- What are the written rules used to process sexual assault claims, and when were these rules were last updated?
- What steps must survivors take to report an assault?
- What are the statistics on how many sexual assault cases have been filed under the university's process over the last five years?

- What is the sex, race, and age breakdown of those who report, those who are being investigated, and those who are found guilty?
- How many survivors have dropped cases short of resolution or have started the process of filing a complaint but not completed it? (and why?)
- How many perpetrators are punished each year; what punishment have they received?

**For law enforcement, ask:**
- How many assaults on campus are reported each month or year?
- What time of day do assaults occur?
- What is the sex, race, and age breakdown of those who report?
- How many survivors have dropped cases short of resolution?
  - or how many survivors have started the process of filing a complaint but not completed it? (and why?)
- What are the locations where assaults have occurred?
- What is the process used to evaluate and process these reports?

**For student groups or the women's center, ask:**
- Do they keep independent statistics on campus sexual assault incidents?
- How do those statistics line up with the university's data?
- What do they hear about the responsiveness of campus police and the fairness of the university process?
- Have they met with the university administrators or law enforcement to raise these issues? If so, have any changes been made to policies or practices?

You will learn a lot by analyzing the information you gather. It can help you decipher the difference between the overall number of assaults that are reported and the number of perpetrators held accountable. When data is studied and interpreted it can pinpoint "hot spots" where assaults occur, and whether there is an adequate law-enforcement presence there. Depending on what you learn, you can ask follow-up questions about what the university is doing to prevent sexual assault, update the process for reporting, or police the campus differently.

Asking these questions also helps you identify others who share your goals. You may find others who have been working to change local or state laws around sexual assault and they can place your advocacy in the context of what they and others are doing. Religious leaders may be part of a coalition addressing this issue, as well as associations of university professors or local business leaders. You may not have previously known about these efforts, but it helps to tie your advocacy into a broader movement, and that puts more pressure on the university.

If you are interested in addressing a broad issue such as climate change, think about where you want to focus your efforts. Is it on legal reform, changing a corporate or workplace policy, or the way that your retirement funds are invested? Once you narrow it down and decide what type of change you seek (See **Framework For Advocacy and Action, Step 1: Identify an Issue You Care About**), then you can begin to identify who the decision-makers are (**Framework for Advocacy and Action, Step 4**), and what you want to ask of them.

If you want to change a company's policy on using palm oil in their products because that affects the environment or because of working conditions, the decision-makers are company executives and board members. The issue is critical given that palm oil is now the most widely used vegetable oil[21] and the methods for farming it contribute significantly to carbon pollution and rainforest destruction.

**The type of questions to ask are:**

- Where does your company get its palm oil?
- What are your practices regarding harvesting palm oil?
- Do you monitor working conditions, particularly for women?
- How do you ensure that children aren't harvesting palm oil that your company uses?
- Have you looked into alternatives such as rapeseed oil, soybean oil, sunflower oil, or olive oil? If not, why not?

You can also use easily available apps[22] to ascertain which consumer products use palm oil, to make purchasing decisions based on what you learn, and to let companies know just that.

### 7. Develop Suggestions for Solving The Challenges You Are Raising

It's important to suggest solutions for the issue you are raising. If you don't, those with power may dismiss you and question your commitment. The solution you propose doesn't have to be perfect, or solve the entire problem. But putting something forward reflects your seriousness and interest in making change. It also gives your effort more focus, which makes it easier for others to organize around it and thus amplify your message.

Using the sexual assault policy example, a message to university administrators and trustees could be:

*"I have heard there is an issue with sexual assault and student safety on campus. I am concerned, as an alumna and a parent of two students studying at the university this fall. I want to make sure that the university has the most fair system for prosecuting sexual assault and protecting survivors. A fair process is good for the university's standing in the broader community. I would like the university to be forward looking, and willing to develop solutions to address an issue that affects many young people, students, and community members, both male and female."*

### 8. Ask Your Questions and Outline Your Suggestions

There are many ways to ask these questions, and you should use the combination that works for you. You can:

- Send a letter or email.
- Engage on social media about your issue with others who share your views, or with decision-makers.
- Ask in person at meetings or if you see the policy maker in person at an event.
- Make an appointment specifically to talk about the issue, ask your questions, and if appropriate be ready with a concrete ask for the meeting. For example, you can ask the person you are meeting with if they will consider a policy change or sponsor relevant legislation (if needed), or ask if they will commit to looking into the issue and consider your suggestion for action on the issue.

## CLOSING THE GENDER PAY GAP

Beginning in 2015, the cloud-based customer-management company **Salesforce reviewed its salary structure** and possible gender pay gaps at the urging of then-President and Chief Personnel Officer **Cindy Robbins**. When she brought the results of the review to **CEO Marc Benioff**'s attention, he was "at first stunned and in denial." As Benioff said later,[23] "It was everywhere . . . every department, every division, every geography." As a result, Benioff ordered that the discrepancies be remedied.[24] Subsequent studies found that 5% of Salesforce's 35,000 global employees required pay adjustments; 39% of those employees were women, 54% were men, and 7% were employees of diverse race and ethnicity.[25]

Or at the very least, ask them if you can return for another meeting in a month to discuss progress.

If you need a script for your conversation, here's a start. You should only address one issue in each phone call, video chat, or letter:

> *Hello, my name is _____, and I am a constituent of President/Governor/Senator _____. I am calling/writing to urge that Senator ___ vote yes (or no) on bill number ___ about [climate change]. Do you know how she will vote?*

**Asking questions forces these institutions to gather data in order to answer you.** Absent a question, people may not know that their firm's policies and practices are discriminatory. A company may know the number of women working as engineers or on-air media personalities, but may never have analyzed whether men and women in the same positions are paid the same amount for the same work.[26] An organization may have never looked at the impact of its hiring practices or considered how interview questions about salary history perpetuate unequal pay for women and others who are marginalized.[27]

Having a concrete suggestion demonstrates your commitment to the issue, and if you've done your homework, the person you are meeting with will at least consider following through on your ideas *in some way*, or will open up a dialogue about how to move forward in another way.

### 9. What's Next? Follow Up!

Once you have taken all of these steps, keep the pressure on decision-makers so that your issue isn't forgotten. In other words, following up is important. This means:

- **MOST IMPORTANT:** Send a thank-you note. In most cases you will want to include a recap of what was discussed.
- Consider working with an "organizing and advocacy partner." This can be a friend or family member who can serve as a sounding board and a collaborator as you strategize and move forward.
- Ask for another meeting (and while you are at it, get to know the staff who support the decision-maker, as they can be helpful in getting that next meeting).
- Monitor the issue and your progress.

## WOMEN'S HISTORY MATTERS

The accomplishments of women like Susan B. Anthony, Sojourner Truth, Marie Curie, Harriet Tubman, Dolores Huerta, Shirley Chisholm, Eleanor Roosevelt, and thousands of others are not taught in schools, and the contributions of these women are not reflected in everything from popular culture to museums to textbooks to litanies of key thinkers. Throughout this book, I highlight women role models, but there are thousands more who have contributed to gender equality.

Understanding women's history helps us learn how women have wielded power and influence, and how they have faced and overcome challenges. Ensuring everyone knows about these women and their roles in history recognizes those who have come before us and shines a light on what is possible for women and girls.

**March 8 is International Women's Day and March is Women's History Month in the U.S.[28]**

- Identify and engage with other individuals who are interested in the issue. Start to organize them to take action.

- Identify and engage with those who can influence the relevant decision-makers on your issue.

- Develop a tracking system if you are trying to get legislation introduced or a policy changed. Include names and pertinent information on:

  - Legislators who are co-sponsors
  - Decision-makers who can change a policy
  - Legislators who (and how many) support you

- Legislators who (and how many) oppose you (this last item is particularly important!)
- Develop an easy way to report to others interested in your issue about progress, via email and/or a public website.

### TAKE ACTION IN YOUR DAILY LIFE!

You may decide that the most important thing you can do is raise awareness at home. If that is the case, then you can engage people at the grassroots level and make the case that people in your community should care about empowering women and girls. Each chapter in *Take Action* will give you some specific suggestions and ideas about how you can start RIGHT NOW to make a difference.

---

# A Framework for Advocacy & Action

**1.**
Identify an issue you care about.

**2.**
Research: Do current laws or programs disadvantage women and/or girls?

**3.**
Investigate the context in order to understand the landscape.

**4.**
Learn who has the power to make changes.

**5.**
Define your interest in this issue.

**6.**
Prepare your questions.

**7.**
Develop suggestions for solving the challenges you are raising.

**8.**
Ask your questions and outline your suggestions.

**9.**
What's next? Follow up!

## And: **Take Action in Your Daily Life!**

---

Liberian President Ellen Johnson-Sirleaf, Liberian activist Leymah Gbowee, and Yemeni activist Tawakkol Karman jointly won the 2011 Nobel Peace Prize.

Marie Curie, the only woman (so far) to have been awarded two Nobel Prizes. Toni Morrison, American Nobel and Pulitzer prize winning author, editor, and professor.

# ROLE MODELS AND TRAILBLAZERS:
# WOMEN NOBEL LAUREATES

Women have received 58 Nobel Prizes, with Marie Curie, the first woman Nobel Laureate, winning twice. Overall, women have received the Nobel Prize across numerous disciplines:

- **Peace (17)**
- **Literature (16)**
- **Medicine (12)**
- **Chemistry (7)**
- **Physics (4)**
- **Economic Studies (2)**[29]

To date, there have been 603 prizes awarded to 962 laureates.[30] The number of women Nobel Laureates is 57. Here are profiles of some of the women who have made history.

**Marie Curie** shared the 1903 Nobel Prize in Physics with her husband, Pierre, for extracting two previously unknown elements from pitchblende, polonium, and radium, both more radioactive than uranium. After she was widowed, she continued the couple's work and was awarded the 1911 Prize in Chemistry for successfully producing radium as a pure metal and documenting properties of radioactive elements and their compounds. In 1935, their daughter, Irène Joliot-Curie, was awarded the Nobel Prize in Chemistry with her husband, Frederic Joliot.

**Toni Morrison** was awarded the 1993 Nobel Prize in Literature for the body of her work revolving around the Black experience. Her works often depict difficult circumstances and the dark side of humanity, but still convey integrity and redemption. Among her works are her debut novel, *The Bluest Eye*, as well as *Song of Solomon* and *Beloved*.

In 2011, the Nobel Prize for Peace was jointly awarded to three women: **President Ellen Johnson-Sirleaf** of Liberia, **Leymah Gbowee**, a Liberian peace activist, and **Tawakkol Karman**, a Yemeni democracy and women's rights activist.

President Johnson-Sirleaf was elected president of Liberia in 2005 and re-elected in 2011. As the first woman head of state ever to be democratically elected in Africa, she worked to promote peace, reconciliation, and social and economic development. Leymah Gbowee organized women from different ethnic and religious groups to fight for peace. Dressed in white T-shirts, they held daily demonstrations at the Monrovia fishmarket. She then led a delegation of Liberian women to Ghana to pressure the warring factions during peace talks, playing a decisive role in ending the civil war. Tawakkol Karman co-founded the group Women Journalists Without Chains in 2005, in order to promote freedom of expression and democratic rights. From 2007 to 2010, she regularly led demonstrations and sit-ins in Tahrir Square, Sana'a, Yemen. She actively participated in the 2011 protests against ruling regimes that took place in a number of Arab countries.

# DIVING DEEP

Here is more in-depth information that you can use to up your ante as an advocate. This section contains other things you can "DO" besides being clear about your goals and asking questions.

## WORKING WITH ESTABLISHED ORGANIZATIONS

Find an organization that works on the issue you care about and get involved. Once you have decided an issue for your advocacy focus, it's important to find an organization that reflects your views and approach to policy advocacy. This section has a list of questions to ask as you search for an "advocacy home." You can also ask friends and neighbors who are already involved. In addition, many large organizations have local chapters, so look for those because they can bring a global or national perspective to work being done at the state or local level.

Here are some things to consider:

### 1. What is the group's mission and vision?

Some organizations address one issue, some have a broader or multi-issue mandate. Does the organization provide direct services, advocate for policy change, and/or develop programs to impact communities? Is it focused on bringing grassroots voices to the table? Convincing elites? What does it want to accomplish? If you cannot find this information online, contact someone who can answer these questions.

# DATA DRIVES POLICY CHANGE

**Sex-disaggregated data** highlights the differing experiences, needs, constraints, and opportunities for women, girls, men, and boys. Data disaggregated by sex is critical to structuring policies and programs.

This means asking "who questions" in a meeting, a call, an email, or a survey:

- Who owns land?
- Who works in a certain job category?
- Who drops out of secondary school?
- Who serves on corporate boards?
- Who is being hired?
- Who goes to engineering or nursing school?
- Who is elected to office?

It also means collecting information about the different ways in which women, men, girls, and boys are treated.

- Are women and men paid differently for the same job?
- Are they promoted at the same rate?
- Do they have the same access to the internet?
- Do girls and boys obtain birth certificates when they are born?
- How often are girls and boys called on by their teachers in the classroom?

**The questions are endless.**

## 2. Does the organization's mission align with your policy or programmatic goals?

Ask why the organization was formed, and what unique constituency or voice it brings to the issue. If you are looking to combat violence against women, does the group represent women who are survivors? Women from a certain segment of the community or a certain age group? Service providers? The business community? It is important to clarify that an organization is not duplicating work that others are doing, or if it is, why the duplication is needed.

## 3. What is the organization's budget and size?

Organizations of different sizes operate differently. Larger, more well-established organizations move more slowly and can be risk-averse, but they often have long histories and deep institutional memory, and they usually operate in larger arenas. Younger organizations can be more flexible and nimble but may not have strong connections with appropriate decision-makers or be as adept at managing funds and filing paperwork. Again, this information should be available online.

## 4. How does the organization select and vet partners?

This matters because it tells you how careful the organization is with regard to its funds and its brand. Ask about the process it uses to obtain information. What kind of due diligence does it conduct, what kind of data does it request from potential and current grantees, and what are its accountability measures?

## 5. How does the organization measure its impact? Does it collect disaggregated data in terms of sex and race?

Make sure to find out what the organization reports about the impact of its work. In the short term, an organization could count the number of men and women who attend a business training, or the number of boys and girls enrolled in school. Mid-term impact would reflect changes in behavior based on the intervention, such as the number of new businesses or the number of children advancing to the next level of schooling. Long-term outcomes can include change in a family's income after a year, higher graduation rates, or social-norm changes.

## 6. Does the organization make its strategic documents easily available?

In the U.S., nonprofits, foundations, and universities are required to report their activities to the Internal Revenue Service each year, using Form 990. This form collects information about the organization's mission, programs, and finances, and provides an opportunity to report on accomplishments. A Form 990 tells you where the organization gets its money and what it pays its employees. Reputable organizations usually make this information available online, so look for it there or ask for a copy.

There are also services –such as Charity Navigator[31]–that evaluate charitable organizations in the U.S., or Global Giving, that provide donors information about vetted, locally driven organizations around the world.[32] Guidestar USA offers a free database of over 2.2 million IRS-recognized non-profits.[33]

## POLICIES AND PRACTICES IN YOUR OWN WORKPLACE

If you are in a decision-making position at your own organization, or if you want to advocate for change, take steps to create a more supportive workplace culture where employees can both do well at work and have a personal life. Small changes make a difference, like closer parking for pregnant employees, more casual dress policies, and being able to bring your pet to work. But more important are policies and procedures guaranteeing a fair pay and promotion system, paid family-leave benefits, job-sharing options, and safe working conditions. If you can help make these happen, do. If you aren't in that kind of role, figure out who is and advocate for these policies.

**Be alert for and don't perpetuate biases against women or anyone who may not feel comfortable speaking up.**

Women's contributions to meetings often aren't acknowledged. Multiple studies conclude that women are interrupted more often in meetings and their ideas taken less seriously than men.[34] We see it in meetings and on award shows (recall Kanye West interrupting Taylor Swift after she won a Grammy). This behavior is so common that there is now a word for it: *mansplaining*, when a man interrupts a woman to explain something that the woman knows more about than he does. If this happens in a meeting, stand up for your colleague by reinforcing what she said and giving her due credit for her idea.

Ask about establishing meeting ground rules to level the playing field:
- Don't allow people to talk over each other
- Go around the room to get everyone's input on a critical decision
- Keep track of who has spoken and call on those who have not before giving someone a second opportunity

If there are issues with people assuming a male subordinate is in charge, or one of your male colleagues takes credit for someone else's ideas, be willing to have an uncomfortable conversation early (and often).

In addition to the gender-pay remediation at Salesforce, CEO Marc Benioff instituted policies to require that 30% of the meeting participants be women,[35] with an express goal to increase women's leadership and likelihood of promotion.

**Do what you can to bring women to the table and into the spotlight.**

We can help young women – or women new to the sector or organization regardless of age – build leadership skills by inviting them to events as our guests, encouraging them to write blogs and articles, suggesting them as speakers on panels, and nominating them for awards. This can help address another gender gap. Less than 15% of the millions of quotes shared every day are quotes attributed to women and girls.[36]

## ROLE MODELS MATTER (a lot)

Both boys and girls establish gender-role stereotypes as early as age two.[37] Even when parents treat children equally, gender norms are perpetuated by characters on screen, aisles of toys that are "appropriate" for girls and not boys (or vice-versa), and casual conversation.

People often ask boys what they want to do when they grow up, while they compliment girls on their clothes and how they look. This has significant consequences when we consider the fact that most children develop an idea of their career interests by middle school.[38]

References to White men – such as Charles Darwin and Gregor Mendel – still dominate in science textbooks and curriculum. While textbooks are becoming more diverse, at the current pace it will take years for textbook mentions to align with who is actually studying science: 28 years for women, 50 years for Asians, 30 years for Hispanics, and up to 500 years for mentions of Blacks.[39]

This is important as many girls attribute their career aspirations to women role models,[40] especially in science, technology, engineering and math (STEM) fields. Young women who are exposed to women scientists, engineers, programmers, coders, and technologists are more likely to

- Receive better grades in STEM classes
- Pursue STEM careers
- Have more confidence in their skills

Seeing women in these jobs also affects the way that boys view what kinds of careers and jobs are suited to women. Since many girls tend to see women's career success in "non-traditional" fields as a matter of luck, rather than something possible to achieve with commitment and focus, it is important that *all* children read about or actually meet women role models who discuss in detail their individual journey, including the challenges they have faced and overcome.[41]

Seeing women in non-traditional jobs in the media also has an impact. At George Mason University, 90% of students in the school's forensic science program are women, and many U.S. police departments report the majority of crime-scene investigators are women.[42] Sixty-three percent of women who are working in STEM today attribute it to watching Dana Scully do her job on the *X-Files*.[43]

**Isis Wenger** started the **#ILookLikeAnEngineer** campaign[44] after people questioned whether she was a model, not an engineer, because she was "too attractive." In response, Wenger posted a photo with the hashtag #ILookLikeAnEngineer and invited others to do the same, generating over 50,000 related photos.

Wenger's campaign has four objectives:

1. Give visibility to and normalize non-stereotypical engineers
2. Increase awareness of discrimination that non-stereotypical engineers face
3. Encourage an atmosphere of diversity, equity, and inclusion in tech
4. Inspire people who may not have considered being engineers before

## THE URGENT NEED TO INCLUDE WOMEN IN
## THE DECISION-MAKING PROCESS

Empowering women means including women by making it convenient for them to participate in the decision-making process. This means helping women and girls become meaningfully engaged in conversations, discussions, and dialogues about laws, policy, neighborhood needs, and problem solving. An effective way to think about this is the phrase "Nothing about them without them." It's as simple as that.

Women must:

- Have access to balanced, objective information upon which decisions about them and their community are being made
- Actively participate in all consultations and meetings
- Actively collaborate and engage with policymakers in each aspect of decision making
- Be empowered to retain control over these important decisions

But most women are "time poor," responsible as they are – even if they also work outside the home – for the majority of household chores, for caregiving, and for procuring and preparing food three times a day. These responsibilities have been highlighted across continents and social spectrums as people shelter in place during the COVID pandemic.

The more time a woman uses for unpaid care work, the less time she has to work outside the home and to take on additional tasks, like attending meetings with elected officials.[45] Women spend at least twice as much time on unpaid care and domestic work than men do. In fact, women's unpaid work is estimated to comprise between 10% and 39% of a country's gross domestic product (GDP).[46] In the U.S., on average, American women spend 2.5 hours a day on household tasks (men spend 1.9 hours) and that does not include childcare.[47] Married American mothers spend almost twice as much time on housework and child care as do married fathers. In fact, these mothers spend more time on child care today than women did 50 years ago.[48]

In some places women do not feel comfortable going out at night or after dark. In others, certain locations are seen as unfriendly to women or unsafe. In many countries, women walk miles and hours to gather firewood and water.

As a result, elected officials and decision-makers need to schedule meetings or town halls at times and in ways that make sense for women. They can use other ways to gather information as well, by:

- Going door-to-door to ask questions
- Reaching out to organizations and groups that women in the community already belong to

- Holding online focus groups or online meetings
- Traveling to places where women congregate, like grocery stores, markets and coffee shops

## CONCLUSION

This chapter developed the **Framework for Advocacy and Action**, which you can use as you learn how to become an effective ally and advocate when working on the issues that you care about. Consider inviting a friend or family member to be your advocacy and organizing partner so you can share progress, help each other during the times of struggle and difficulty, and share the wins. This can be an effective strategy even if you join an already formed group or organization, which I strongly advise that you do.

The next four chapters outline issues in key areas – education, the economy, gender-based violence, and the power of politics – and give you facts and figures that you can use to make a compelling case for change. Each chapter outlines questions to ask to prompt discussion, conversations, and change; includes both a section titled Diving Deep and a list of Resources to help you become a fledgling expert on each topic; and in general is designed to give you enough information to start you on your way as an effective agent of change.

**Together, we can do it. We can build a better world for women and girls.**

# RESOURCES: Advocacy & Activism
## Information Is Power

In every chapter of the book you will find a list of resources that you can refer to when you are formulating your initial questions, doing your research, finding out who has the power to make change, and preparing your questions and making a plan of advocacy. Here you will find resources to help you learn about becoming an effective ally and advocate.

These lists are available/updated at: stepheniefoster.com

## Movies and TV

- **Carla Hayden (2016)**. A very short video about Carla Hayden, the 14th Librarian of Congress. She is the first woman and the first Black person to serve in this role.

- **Erin Brockovich (2000)**. A dramatization of the story of Erin Brockovich, who fought against energy corporation Pacific Gas and Electric and won. Starring Julia Roberts, who won the Academy Award for her portrayal.

- **The Fight (2020)**. Chronicles cases brought by the American Civil Liberties Union around voting rights and reproductive rights. Narrated by Kerry Washington.

- **Harlan County, USA (1976)**. Documentary about the labor tensions in the coal mining industry in rural Kentucky.

- **Harriet (2019)**. The story of Harriet Tubman, American abolitionist and a formerly enslaved woman, starring Cynthia Erivo and Janelle Monáe (she/her/they), and directed by Kasi Lemmons, a Black director.

- **The Hate U Give (2018)**. The story of Starr Carter, who is torn between the poor, mostly Black neighborhood in which she lives and the wealthy, mostly White prep school she attends. This film follows the fallout after she witnesses a police shooting of her close friend. Based on the book by the same name.

- **Heather Booth: Changing the World (2016)**. Organizer and activist Heather Booth began her remarkable career at the height of the civil rights movement. While chronicling her life and work, this film explores pivotal moments in progressive movements over the last fifty years, including Fannie Lou Hamer and the Freedom Summer Project, as well as Booth's founding of the JANE Underground in 1964.

- **The Immortal Life of Henrietta Lacks (2017)**. HBO movie based on Rebecca Skloot's book by the same name about Lacks, whose cervical cancer cells changed the course of cancer treatment and the lingering issues of medical ethics and race.

- **Iron Jawed Angels (2004)**. The story of women who risked their lives for women's right to vote. Starring Hilary Swank, Anjelica Huston, and Vera Farmiga.

- **Just Mercy (2019)**. A biographical legal drama about Walter McMillian, who appeals a wrongful murder conviction with the help of Bryan Stevenson. Based on the memoir of the same name written by Stevenson, starring Michael B. Jordan and Jamie Foxx.

- **LaDonna Harris: Indian 101 (2014).** This film celebrates Comanche activist and national civil rights leader LaDonna Harris, who has influenced Native and mainstream American history since the 1960s. Filmmaker Julianna Brannum, Harris's great-grandniece, chronicles the struggles which led Harris to become a voice for Native people, as well as her contemporary work strengthening and rebuilding indigenous communities.

- **Maggie Growls (2002).** A portrait of Maggie Kuhn (1905-1995), who founded the leading senior advocacy organization, the Gray Panthers, after being forced to retire at the age of 65. Her outrage and determination fueled a chain reaction that changed the lives of older Americans, repealing mandatory retirement laws and proving that "old" is not a dirty word.

- **13th (2016).** Filmmaker Ava DuVernay explores the history of racial inequality in the U.S., focusing on the fact that the nation's prisons are disproportionately filled with Blacks. The film is named after the 13th Amendment to the U.S. Constitution, which ended slavery.

- **Unbreathable: The Fight for Healthy Air (2020).** This short film focuses on the remarkable progress in cleaning up air pollution and saving lives driven by the Clean Air Act, and the obstacles that remain when it comes to ensuring healthy air for all communities. Directed by Maggie Burnette Stogner and produced by Elizabeth Herzfeldt-Kamprath.

## Books

- *Barbara Jordan: American Hero* (**1998**) by Mary Beth Rogers. Biography of the first Black woman to serve in the Texas Senate after Reconstruction and the first Black woman elected to Congress from the South.

- *The Blue Sweater: Bridging the Gap Between Rich and Poor in an Interconnected World* (**2009**) by Jacqueline Novogratz. Autobiography of a woman who left international banking to dedicate her life to understanding global poverty. Believing that traditional charity often fails, Novogratz finds philanthropic investing helps people become self-sufficient and changes lives.

- *Half the Sky: Turning Oppression into Opportunity for Women Worldwide* (**2010**) by Nicholas Kristof and Sheryl WuDunn. Through the stories of women across the globe, the Pulitzer Prize winning authors show how the key to economic progress worldwide is to help women find their economic potential.

- *In the Shadow of Statues: A White Southerner Confronts History* (**2018**) by Mitch Landrieu. Story of how and why this New Orleans mayor removed four Confederate statues and helped continue a national debate on institutional racism and inequality.

- *The MoveOn Effect: The Unexpected Transformation of American Political Advocacy* (**2012**) by David Karpf. A political scientist and political organizer, Karpf writes a detailed account of the internet's impact on American politics, progressive political associations, and the role of the average American citizen in this new era of political mobilization.

- *My Life on the Road* (2015) by Gloria Steinem. A memoir of Steinem's life and how her travel has impacted the way she sees the world, her activism, and her leadership.

- *No One is Too Small to Make a Difference* (2019) by Greta Thunberg. A collection of 11 speeches by the 15-year-old who sparked a global movement on climate change.

- *Use the Power You Have: A Brown Woman's Guide to Politics and Political Change* (2020) by U.S. Representative Pramila Jayapal. Memoir of an activist turned Congresswoman that offers ideas and inspiration for engaging and advocating, whether locally or nationally.

- *Unbowed: A Memoir* (2006) by Wangari Maathai. The Nobel Prize winner recounts her journey from childhood in rural Kenya to founding the Green Belt Movement. Jailed and beaten on numerous occasions, Maathai fought tirelessly to save Kenya's forests and to restore democracy.

- *We Should All Be Feminists* (2014) by Chimamanda Ngozi Adichie. Drawing extensively on her own experiences and her understanding of sexual politics, the author explores what it means to be a woman and why we should all be feminists.

- *Wish You Happy Forever: What China's Orphans Taught Me About Moving Mountains* (2014) by Jenny Bowen. A memoir of how the author went from reading an article on the thousands of girls in China's orphanages to adopting a child and creating the Half the Sky Foundation to help orphaned girls in China.

## Organizations

- **Belmont-Paul Women's Equality National Monument**
  Home to the National Woman's Party (NWP), this building has been at the epicenter of the struggle for women's rights, serving as headquarters for the massive political effort to obtain the right to vote, and a second home for the women of the organization. From this house the NWP developed innovative strategies and tactics to advocate for the ERA and equality for women. President Barack Obama designated the house as a national monument. https://www.nps.gov/bepa/index.htm

- **Gender Avenger**
  Gender Avenger's mission is to ensure women are represented in the public dialogue. You can use the Gender Avenger app to monitor the makeup of panels at conferences and meetings you attend. www.genderavenger.com

- **Kota Alliance**
  The Kota Alliance is a nonprofit social enterprise incubator in New York City that provides fiscal, physical, and programmatic support to startup civil

society organizations and women-centered enterprises whose work increases gender equality and empowers women and girls, locally and globally. https://www.kota-alliance.org/

- **National Partnership for Women & Families**
  The Partnership's goal is to improve the lives of women through equality, with a focus on advocating for women's health, reproductive rights, and economic justice. It is a national nonprofit, non-partisan organization working to change policy and culture through advocacy in both the public and private sectors at the federal, state, and local levels. www.nationalpartnership.org

- **National Women's History Alliance (NWHA)**
  The NWHA is the preeminent resource for information and material about the role of women in American history. Every year, the NWHA coordinates observances of National Women's History Month and in conjunction with academic institutions, holds workshops and conferences that highlight the role of women in particular areas, such as the Women of the West. www.nationalwomenshistoryalliance.org

- **National Women's Law Center (NWLC)**
  NWLC fights for gender justice — in the courts, in public policy, and in our society — by working on issues central to the lives of women and girls. NWLC uses the law to change culture, drive solutions, and break down barriers, especially for those who face multiple forms of discrimination, including women of color, LGBTQ people, and low-income women and families. www.nwlc.org

- **She the People**
  She the People brings together a national network of women of color – voters, organizers, movement builders, elected leaders – to transform democracy. The organization is based on shared values of justice and inclusivity, and in swing states in the South, Southwest, and Midwest, aims to increase the voter turn-out of women of color. www.shethepeople.org

- **UltraViolet**
  UltraViolet is a rapidly growing community of people mobilized to fight sexism and create a more inclusive world that accurately represents all women, from politics and government to media and pop culture. Through strategic advocacy, UltraViolet works to improve the lives of women and girls of all identities and backgrounds, and all people impacted by sexism, by dismantling discrimination and creating a cost for sexism. www.weareultraviolet.org

- **Women's Funding Network (WFN)**
  WFN is the largest philanthropic network in the world devoted to women and girls. The network of more than 100 women's funds and foundations in 14 countries is committed to solving critical social issues – such as poverty and global security – through the financial power of its influences and funders, all focused on gender equity. www.womensfundingnetwork.org

These lists are available/updated at: stepheniefoster.com

# NOTES

1 Crenshaw, Kimberlé, "Mapping the Margins: Intersectionality, Identity Politics, and Violence Against Women of Color," https://bit.ly/3msgm3t.

2 https://nwlc.org/wp-content/uploads/2021/01/December-Jobs-Day.pdf

3 Speech by Greta Thunberg, "I'm Too Young to do This," February 2, 2018.

4 Time Magazine, "Greta Thunberg: Time Person of the Year 2019," https://bit.ly/3odwhTA.

5 "History of Women's Participation in Clinical Research," National Institutes of Health, https://bit.ly/37gURfG.

6 "Happy 25th Birthday, OWHR!," National Institutes of Health, https://bit.ly/3qdQ5s3.

7 "Nicotine Therapy More Effective for Men than Women, Says Research," Science Daily, https://bit.ly/2Vkis9I.

8 Greenberger, Phyllis, "Pain Relievers Work Differently in Men and Women," ABC News, March 26, 2002, https://abcn.ws/2Vlcm96.

9 In 2013, the U.S. Food and Drug Administration sharply cut its recommended dosages of Ambien for women, after years of complaints about grogginess and falling asleep while driving. Tests showed that women metabolized the active ingredient much more slowly than men. See Falkenberg, Kai, "FDA Takes Action on Ambien; Concedes Women at Greater Risk," Forbes, https://bit.ly/3losCR9.

10 Hollon, Tom, "From Freedom Ride to Gender-based Biology," The Scientist, October 29, 2000. https://bit.ly/3msmloQ.

11 Biddle, Matthew, "Men are still more likely than women to be perceived as leaders, study finds," University of Buffalo News Center, August 6, 2018, https://bit.ly/3loNyHZ.

12 Germano, Maggie, "Women are Working More Than Ever, But They Still Take On Most Household Responsibilities," Forbes, March 27, 2019, https://bit.ly/3lsElOx.

13 Vargas, Theresa, "A 9-year-old Girl Got People to Finally Stop Thinking of the Peach-Colored Crayon as the 'Skin-Color' Crayon," The Washington Post, February 22, 2020, https://wapo.st/36lelk6.

14 Page, Sydney, "A Medical Student Couldn't Find How Symptoms Look on Darker Skin. He Decided to Publish a Book About It.," The Washington Post, July 22, 2020, https://wapo.st/3qaNBuB.

15 Slack, Megan, "From the Archives: President Obama Signs the Lilly Ledbetter Fair Pay Act," The White House, January 30, 2012, https://bit.ly/3qhlolR.

16 "Why Climate Change Disproportionately Affects Women," Global Citizen, https://bit.ly/33x7PVr.

17 Iglesias, Carlos, "The Gender Gap in Internet Access: Using a women-centered method," Web Foundation, March 10, 2020, https://bit.ly/33rYbmT.

18 Auxier, Brooke and Anderson, Monica, "As Schools Close Due to the Coronavirus, Some U.S. Students Face a Digital 'Homework Gap'," Pew Research Center, March 16, 2020, https://pewrsr.ch/39qcDjj.

19 "Digital Divide in the United States," https://bit.ly/3qdT6Zi.

20 Deduck, "Powermap Example," Wikipedia Commons, https://bit.ly/2Jg6oUG.

21 See Rainforest Action Network, https://bit.ly/2Vm7twk.

22 Wilson-Powell, Georgina, "This App Detects Palm Oil in Products," Pebble Magazine, January 3, 2019, https://bit.ly/33xFpe9.

23 Swantes, Marcel, "The CEO of Salesforce Found Out His Female Employees Were Paid Less Than Men. His Response Is a Priceless Leadership Lesson," Inc., July 26, 2018, https://bit.ly/3oe9w2b.

24 Ibid.

25 Cindy Robbins, 2019 Salesforce Equal Pay Update, Salesforce Blog, April 2, 2019, https://sforce.co/2VjYfAN.

26 "Gender Pay Gap: What is the pay gap where I work?" BBC News, April 5, 2019, https://bbc.in/3lm3tXd.

27  California, Delaware, Massachusetts, Oregon, and Puerto Rico, as well as major cities like New York, New Orleans, Pittsburgh and Philadelphia have made it illegal to ask the question: "What is your current salary?" These laws require managers to state a position's compensation based on the applicant's worth to their company to ensure that lower wages, which are historically provided to women and minorities, do not follow them throughout their careers.

28  History.com Editors, "Women's History Month 2021," History.com, updated February 28, 2020, https://bit.ly/37nViF6.

29  "The Nobel Prizes Awarded to Women," The Nobel Prize, https://bit.ly/3fQ0Ewu.

30  "All Nobel Prizes," The Nobel Prize, https://bit.ly/3fPWCV3.

31  www.charitynavigator.com

32  www.globalgiving.org

33  www.guidestar.org

34  Brinlee, Morgan, "Yup, Research Says Women Are Interrupted Way More Than Men," Bustle, June 15, 2017, https://bit.ly/37h1Sgw.

35  Swantes, Marcel, "The CEO of Salesforce Found Out His Female Employees Were Paid Less Than Men. His Response Is a Priceless Leadership Lesson," Inc., July 26, 2018, https://bit.ly/3oe9w2b.

36  Research conducted by Quotabelle, summarized at https://bit.ly/2JnZKvl.

37  Rafferty, Jason, "Gender Identity Development in Children," American Academy of Pediatrics, last updated September 18, 2018, https://bit.ly/33viEXY.

38  Shapiro, Mary, "Dreaming Big: What's Gender Got to Do with It? The Impact of Gender Stereotypes on Career Aspirations of Middle Schoolers," CGO Insights, Simmons School of Management, October 2012, https://bit.ly/33v3an6.

39  Brookshire, Bethany, "References to White Men Still Dominate College Biology Text books, Survey Says," The Washington Post, July 26, 2020, https://wapo.st/2KLFCDM.

40  Lockwood, Penelope, "'Someone Like Me Can Be Successful': Do College Students Need Same-Gender Role Models?" Psychology of Women Quarterly 30, no. 1, March 2006, available at https://bit.ly/37pZJ1U. and Nixon, Lucia A., and Robinson, Michael D., "The Educational Attainment of Young Women: Role Model Effects of Female High School Faculty," Demography 36, no. 2, 1999, available at https://bit.ly/2KJDyfx.

41  Ibid.

42  Chandler, Michael Alison, "Women at Forefront of Booming Forensic Science," Washington Post Magazine, August 2, 2012, https://wapo.st/39xikMi. See also, Serra, Cheryl L., "CSI in Real Life," WILMA Magazine, July 1, 2019, https://bit.ly/2HRO0k2.

43  Hornaday, Ann, "Geena Davis Just Made Children's TV More Feminist," The Washington Post, September 19, 2019, https://wapo.st/3qcKNwN.

44  The #ILookLikeAnEngineer Campaign, https://bit.ly/3fP1NVg.

45  Ferrant, Gaëlle et al, "Unpaid Care Work: The missing link in the analysis of gender gaps in labour outcomes," OECD Development Centre, December 2014, https://bit.ly/3lmS FrZ.

46  "Why Care Matters for Social Development," United Nations Research Institute for Social Development Research and Policy Brief 9, February 2010, https://bit.ly/39BxobE.

47  "American Time Use Survey - 2019 Results," Bureau of Labor Statistics, June 25, 2020, https://bit.ly/3o5wCaU.

48  Rao, Aliya Hamid, "Even Breadwinning Wives Don't Get Equality at Home," The Atlantic, May 12, 2019, https://bit.ly/3fPXxVz.

CHAPTER TWO

# It Starts in the Classroom

*"Let us pick up our books and our pens," I said "They are our most powerful weapons. One child, one teacher, one book and one pen can change the world"*

Malala Yousafzai
Nobel Laureate and author

Ensuring that girls everywhere start school and complete their education is as close to a silver bullet as we have to create prosperous, stable, and sustainable communities and countries. Education is a fundamental right,[1] and when girls stay in school they gain the knowledge, skills, and critical thinking abilities that provide them with the tools to effectively make their own life choices.

Keeping girls in school helps eradicate poverty, leads to economic prosperity and growth, and builds stronger and healthier families.[2] We know that better educated women:

- Are healthier,[3]
- Participate at higher rates in the formal labor market and earn more money,[4]
- Are more productive at work and better paid,[5] and
- Have fewer, healthier, and better educated children.[6]

As Americans, we take it for granted that girls and young women will attend and excel in school. In the U.S., 90% of young women graduate from high school and 37% of women from college.[7]

But in other parts of the world, not all young women and girls have access to education. Some girls never set foot in a school and some only attend for a few years. While there has been significant progress in girls' education over the last decades, more work is needed. Between 1970 and 1992, combined primary and secondary enrollment for girls in developing countries rose from 38% to 68%.[8] But today, even before the COVID-19 pandemic, about 62 million girls are not enrolled in school,[9] with this lack of access especially pronounced in Sub-Saharan Africa and

## WOMEN AND STUDENT LOAN DEBT

Since the 1990s, almost 60% of U.S. undergraduates have been women, and more women are pursuing advanced degrees than ever before.[10] This translates to more opportunity but to more debt, as **women hold two-thirds of student-loan debt**. Proposals to cancel *a set dollar amount*, as opposed to a *percentage*, of college debt discriminate against women, who have more student debt. This affects women across demographics as two-thirds of millennials have some kind of postsecondary training.[11]

some parts of South Asia.[12]

The COVID-19 pandemic places these gains at serious risk. Since the global shutdown in March 2020, 1.5 billion students have been pulled out of schools, including 111 million in developing and poor countries.[13] Due to the pandemic, in Africa alone over 250 million primary and secondary children do not attend school.[14] These disruptions are expected to delay the education of 20 million girls in secondary school,[15] and threaten continuing gains for girls' education for the foreseeable future. Lengthy closures can mean some students will never return to school, especially girls.

While girls face different challenges and barriers to their education depending on where they live, it's important to fight for educational equality both in the U.S. *and* in other countries. Everywhere, girls face multiple barriers to education:

- Poverty and family income
- Geographical isolation
- Ethnic and minority status
- Early marriage and/or pregnancy
- Gender-based violence (GBV)

Social norms about what types of subjects girls and young women "should" study are prevalent everywhere.[16] And, in some places, attitudes about the roles of girls and women mean that girls' education isn't a priority. Many families with limited resources educate their sons – not their daughters – believing that boys need education in order to be better equipped to work and support a family, and that education is wasted on girls, who will marry at an early age and move to live with their husband's family.[17]

## WHEN GIRLS ARE EDUCATED, THE BENEFIT IS WIDESPREAD

Education and economic growth are correlated in both developed and developing countries.[18] Women with secondary education see increases in earning power, and will make almost twice as much as women with no education.[19]

The costs to countries of not educating girls is between $15 trillion and $30 trillion in lost lifetime productivity and earnings.[20] If just 10% more adolescent girls attend school, on average a country's GDP will increase by 3%.[21] For example, if India enrolled just one percent more girls in secondary school, the country's GDP would rise by $5.5 billion.[22]

Climate change is also mitigated when girls are educated. Data indicates that a woman with 12 years of education typically has four to five *fewer* children than a woman with no education.[23] Having just one less child reduces carbon emissions by 58.6 tons each year.[24] At the same time, these families and communities are more resilient when confronted with climate-related disasters, and are better able to adapt to the effects of climate change.[25]

---

# A LEARNING GAP

Even though most countries provide primary education:

- 31 million girls of primary school age globally do not attend school.[26]
- 17 million of these girls are never expected to attend school.[27]

In some countries, the raw numbers are staggering:

- In Nigeria, 5 million girls are *not* in school [28]
- In Pakistan, over 3 million girls are *not* attending school.[29]

Even when girls do attend primary school, they drop out at higher rates than boys,[30] accelerating the "learning gap" between boys and girls.

- 34 million girls and young women globally are not enrolled in secondary school.[31]
- In conflict-countries, 90% of adolescent girls are more likely to be out of secondary school than adolescent girls in non-conflict countries.[32]

Lack of schooling has a long-term spillover impact.[33]

- Two-thirds of the 774 million adults who are illiterate are women, a proportion that has remained unchanged for decades.[34]

---

## GIRL-FOCUSED SCHOOLS

All-girls schools can make a difference. A recent U.S. study found that students in all-girls public schools have increased their educational scores, particularly in math and science.[35] Examples include the Ann Richards School for Young Women Leaders in Austin, Texas, and the Young Women's Leadership School of East Harlem, New York.[36]

There are also examples of girl-focused schools across the globe. In Kenya, the Kakenya Centers for Excellence, created by the non-profit organization Kakenya's Dream, takes a girl-centered approach to education.[37] Alumni receive mentoring, scholarships, tutoring, career advice, and assistance applying to universities around the world. As a condition of enrollment, parents must agree their daughters won't be subjected to female genital mutilation/cutting (FGM/C) or forced into marriage.

Situated in a part of Kenya where 80% of Maasai girls leave school by age 12, nearly 80% undergo FGM/C, and over 50% marry before age 19.[38] Kakenya's Dream has so far educated over 500 girls at their boarding schools, supported more than 200 girls continuing on to high school and university, and trained nearly 14,000 boys, girls, and community members on issues of health and human rights. All of the girls finish school, none of them undergo FGM/C, and none of them are married as children.[39] The organization's founder, Dr. Kakenya Ntaiya, is from the 10,000-person village where the school and the other programs are located. An

Dr. Kakenya Ntaiya, founder of The Kakenya Centers.

educator and activist who survived FGM/C and escaped an arranged child-marriage, she is the first woman from her community to attend college in the U.S. Like Malala Yousafzai, Dr. Ntaiya is a role model for her continued focus on, and commitment to, girls' education.

## ADVOCACY AND ACTION: WHAT'S THE FIRST STEP?

In Chapter One, I identified the **Framework for Advocacy and Action**. Let's use that framework in terms of advocacy and organizing for girls' education.

### 1. Identify An Issue You Care About

The focus for this chapter is keeping girls in school so they can learn, make contributions to their families and communities, and have access to every opportunity possible. As an advocate, you can narrow this to focus, for instance, on girls' access to secondary education globally, or focus on a particular country of interest. Narrowing your focus sharpens your goals and makes the rest of the work easier to accomplish and act upon.

### 2. Research: Do Current Laws or Programs Disadvantage Women and Girls?

Once you have a focus, find out if there are laws, policies or practices that impede girls' access to secondary education, or whether and what programs make it more difficult for girls to attend school. **Are there roadblocks you can help dismantle?**

### 3. Investigate the Context So You Can Understand the Landscape

While every country is different, and individual states in the U.S. have their own set of laws and rules, we know that keeping girls in school helps eradicate poverty, leads to economic prosperity and growth, and translates into stronger and healthier families. Contact appropriate agencies or study their websites. Are there proposed policies that can help keep girls in school? (See **Diving Deep** for some examples of what we know works.)

### 4. Find Out Who Has the Power to Make Change

Let's say you want to focus on the need to eliminate or reduce school fees for girls at the secondary level. **Create a power map** (see Chapter 1, Step 4) to figure out who has power to deal with that issue. It could be someone on the local school board or city council, or a politician in the state legislature (in which case you would contact that office). It could be an administrator in the local school system or someone in another local governing body. In all likelihood, it's a combination of these people and institutions.

Information about who is on the City Council or School Board, when it meets, and relevant contact information should be publicly available on government websites.[40] Once you know when meetings occur, you can attend one to get a feel for how the council or board conducts business, what the room looks like, and other details.

Don't worry about finding the "perfect" person to speak with, find someone who has authority on the topic, and contact that person. You'll be asking them the most basic question on your list, which is: "Can you help me in my efforts to eliminate or reduce school fees for girls at the secondary level?" If they say no, ask them if they know someone who *can* help you.

### 5. Define Your Interest in This Issue

Once you have identified your issue, and know who has the power to make the necessary changes, it is important to communicate to the person you will be talking to **why this issue is important enough to trigger your actions**. Be clear, concise/short, concrete/understandable, and convincing. (See Chapter 1, Step 5.)

### 6. Prepare Your Questions

Before you ask the powers-that-be questions about how to eliminate or reduce school fees, be prepared, for example, to make the case that education leads to better jobs.

- Use the research that demonstrates girls'-school enrollment can increase significantly – without subsidies or financial assistance – when families understand that education increases the likelihood that their daughter will get a job.[41]

- In the U.S., women with a bachelor's degree earn about double the wages of their co-workers without a college education, although there is still a gender pay gap.[42]

- In India, information about available white-collar jobs that require skills – such as English, computers, math, and literacy – significantly increased girls' school enrollment.[43] Parents invested substantially more money in their daughters' schooling when parents attended women-only information sessions, and jobs were specifically advertised for women with secondary school education. In addition, girls in those families delayed marriage and childbearing and were given more to eat at home.[44]

- Similarly, in Madagascar and the Dominican Republic, providing information about the types of jobs available by education level and the potential wages increased school attendance rates and test scores for young women.[45]

- Review the information in **Diving Deep** (below).
- Review the material suggested in the **Resources** section of this chapter (remember: INFORMATION IS POWER!).

Here are some specific questions you can ask **teachers and school administrators:**

- What is the breakdown (by sex) of students in your school?
- What is the breakdown (by sex) of teachers?
- How are you addressing gender stereotypes in your lessons?
- What actions have you taken to encourage girls to pursue STEM (science, technology, engineering, and mathematics)
- If a private school: Do you have tuition assistance or scholarships? What is the breakdown of those receiving such assistance?
- How many opportunities are there for girls/young women to play competitive sports?
- Do you equally fund men's and women's teams?
- How far do most students live from your school?
- How do students travel to school?
- How do you ensure that your school is free from violence, harassment, and bullying?

If you are concerned about girls' education in other countries, "asking questions" might look a whole lot more like "reading books and studying websites," than contacting school teachers and administrators in person.

## 7. Develop Suggestions for Solving the Challenges You Are Raising

It's important to suggest solutions for the issue you are raising. If you don't, those with power may dismiss you and question your commitment. **The solution you propose doesn't have to be perfect, or solve the entire problem.** But putting *something* forward reflects your seriousness and interest in making change. It also gives your effort more focus, which makes it easier for others to organize around it and thus amplify your message. Here are some ideas to get you going:

- If you are concerned that not all students have computers at home or access to broadband,[46] you can propose that the school provide every student with a device and/or free broadband access. In the U.S., as we face the COVID-19 pandemic, the Federal Communications Commission issued the Keep Americans Connected Pledge, which asks internet service providers to not disconnect the accounts of consumers who are unable to pay their bills for the next 60 days, to waive late fees, and to open up Wi-Fi hotspots across the country. Companies such as AT&T, CenturyLink, and Verizon signed on.[47]
- If you are concerned about girls' safety at school, organize for girls' safe spaces at schools, for locks on bathroom doors, and for more women teachers and school administrators.

## 8. Ask Your Questions and Outline Your Suggestions

There are many ways to ask the questions you've developed, and you should use the combination that works for you. You can:

- Send a letter or email.

- Engage on social media about your issue with others who share your views, or with decision-makers.
- Ask in person at meetings or if you see the policymaker in person at an event.
- Make an appointment specifically to talk about the issue, ask your questions, and if appropriate be ready with a concrete ask for the meeting. For example, you can ask the person you are meeting with if they will consider a policy change or sponsor relevant legislation (if needed), or ask if they will commit to looking into the issue and consider your suggestion for action on the issue. **Or at the very least, ask them if you can meet again to discuss progress.**

If you need a script for your conversation, here's a start. You should only address one issue in each phone call, video chat, or letter:

> *Hello, my name is _____, and I am a constituent of President/Governor/Senator _____. I am calling/writing to urge that Senator ___ vote yes (or no) on bill number ___ , about girls' access to education. Do you know how she will vote?*

Asking questions forces these institutions to gather data in order to answer you. Absent a question, people may not know that girls and young women at their school are constantly sexually harassed, or that they are dissuaded from enrolling in STEM classes. A school may know the number of students in STEM classes, and even break that down by sex, but not pay attention to the breakdown by age, race, or ethnicity. Teachers may see that girls don't use a certain hallway, but not know it is because they are harassed when walking there.

Having a concrete suggestion demonstrates your commitment to the issue, and if you've done your homework, the person you are meeting with will at least consider following through on your ideas *in some way*, or will open up a dialog about how to move forward in another way.

### 9. What's Next? Follow Up!

Once you have taken all of these steps, keep the pressure on decision-makers so that your issue isn't forgotten. In other words, following up is important. This means:

- **MOST IMPORTANT:** Send a thank-you note. In most cases you will want to include a recap of what was discussed.
- Consider working with an "organizing and advocacy partner." This can be a friend or family member who can serve as a sounding board and a collaborator as you strategize and move forward.
- More than likely there will be a number of actions you can take after your initial meeting. Work with your advocacy partner or with the organization you are working with on the issue to come up with a plan of action.
- Ask for another meeting (remember to get to know the staff who support the decision-maker as they can be helpful in setting up that next meeting).
- Monitor the issue and your progress.
- Identify and engage with other individuals who are interested in the issue. Start to organize them to take action.
- Identify and engage with those who can influence the relevant decision-makers on your issue.
- Develop a tracking system if you are trying to get legislation introduced or a

policy changed. Include names and pertinent information on:

- Legislators who are co-sponsors
- Decision-makers who can change policy
- Legislators who (and how many) support you
- Legislators who (and how many) oppose you (this last item is particularly important!)

- Develop an easy way to report to others interested in keeping girls in school about progress, via email, social media, and/or a public website.

## TAKE ACTION IN YOUR DAILY LIFE!

You may decide that the most important thing you can do is raise awareness at home. If that is the case, then you can engage people at the grassroots level and make the case that people in your community should care about the issue of girls' education and keeping girls in school.

### 1. RAISE AWARENESS! Host a movie screening of films about girls' education.

You can screen *He Named Me Malala*,[48] *Girl Rising*,[49] and others made by or about girls around the world.[50] Bring in a speaker, either in person or by video. Find out if there is someone in your local community who knows about the importance of girls' education first hand. There are lots of organizations focused on this issue and they can help you find a compelling speaker. If you have a child in school, ask her teacher if your child's class (or the entire school) can watch a movie or read a book about girls' education. Here's a good list.[51] (See the **Resources** section at the end of this chapter for more ideas on movies and books.)

### 2. BE AN INTERRUPTER! Confront gender stereotyping at school and at home.

Teachers and books can reinforce gender norms and stereotypes in many ways, usually unconsciously. This ranges from books that show girls and women in only traditional jobs and roles – such as teachers, nurses, and household workers – to teachers who call on boys in class more often than girls. It can also mean discouraging girls from STEM study and boys from nursing or art and design. Encourage girls to join groups that focus on key skills, like *Girls Who Code*[52] and *Black Girls Code*.[53] If you hear that girls and boys are being dissuaded from career paths or classes based on these outdated gender norms, contact the teacher and the school and explain why this is an issue. Write an email, make a phone call, and encourage others to do the same.

### 3. Compliment girls on their intellect and smarts, not just their looks.

Gender norms form in children between the ages of three and seven,[54] when they acquire strong gender biases about the types of jobs men and women should fulfill. Teachers, for example, more often praise girls for their caring behaviors and boys for their physical strength, or influence children to select what they consider to be "gender-appropriate" toys and play materials.[55] Organizations like the Forum for African Women Educationalists, and many more, are now developing toolkits[56] to address these stereotypes and help teachers make sure they aren't perpetuating them.

### 4. Support girl-oriented programs.

These types of programs drive leadership skills at a young age. Encourage your daughters to sign up and cheer them on so they stay involved. Donate funds. Be a troop leader or join a corporate council supporting the Girl Scouts, Girls Inc., or the Radical Monarchs. Ask about being a mentor or coach to girls and young women in these types of groups. (See the **Resources** section later in the chapter for more information.)

## SUMMARY

This chapter outlines how girls' access to education is limited in many places, what gender norms and constraints are at play, and what impact keeping girls from school has on the girls, their families, and their communities.

In addition to the **Framework for Advocacy and Action**, which offers detailed information about how you can effectively advocate for ensuring that all girls have access to education, **Take Action In Your Daily Life** has some concrete suggestions about how to engage friends and family on the grassroots level in an effort to convince them of the importance of girls' education.

# DIVING DEEP

You've learned how important it is to keep girls in school across the globe. Here is more in-depth information that you can use to up your ante as an advocate on this issue. This section contains information on WHAT WE KNOW WORKS to keep girls in school, and on proven strategies that support girls' education.

## WHAT WORKS TO KEEP GIRLS IN SCHOOL?

Use your understanding of what can work as the basis of your advocacy and organizing.

### 1. Eliminate or reduce school fees and costs.

Tuition, fees, and costs are substantial barriers to education for girls.[57] Addressing this issue is especially important with regard to secondary education, which is significantly more expensive than primary education and has a larger impact on long-term earnings, health, gender equality, and civic and political participation. Globally, because of costs and social norms, fewer girls attend secondary school than boys. Here are examples of how eliminating or reducing fees and costs has had an impact:

- In Kenya, girls who received free school uniforms were less likely to get married, become pregnant, or drop out of school.[58]
- In Uganda, providing school meals helped increase girls' attendance and reduced dropout rates.[59]
- In Ghana, providing scholarships for teenage girls led to girls delaying marriage and pregnancy.[60]

### 2. Locate schools closer to girls' homes.

In many countries, the distance that a girl must travel to school is a barrier to her education, as she often travels on unsafe roads and can be exposed to harassment, violence, sexual assault, or abduction.[61] This is more pronounced in rural areas, where there are fewer schools and children must travel longer distances to school.[62] In Tanzania, 23% of young women aged 13 to 24 reported at least one incident of sexual violence traveling to or from school.[63] Here are some examples of how locating schools closer to where girls live has had an impact:

- In Egypt, more than twice as many girls attended school when the school was within one kilometer of her home, as opposed to three kilometers.[64]
- In Afghanistan, girls' enrollment fell by 19% for each additional mile girls lived from school (as opposed to boys, whose enrollment fell by 13%). Every additional mile of travel also had an impact on a girl's test performance.[65]
- In India, enrollment increased by 41%, and the gender gap in enrollment was reduced by almost half, when girls aged 14 were provided a bicycle.[66] This reduced travel time as well as vulnerability to harassment and attacks.

### 3. Use cash incentives to keep girls in school.

Conditional cash transfers (CCTs) are payments conditioned on certain behaviors, such as enrolling children in schools, getting regular medical check-ups, or receiving vaccinations. CCTs tie cash payments, or another valuable resource such as livestock, to these actions. These programs are most effective if they start early and continue until the end of middle or secondary school.[67] Here are some examples of how CCTs have had an impact:

- In Brazil, CCTs encouraged families to send their children to school and to engage in preventive healthcare, such as immunizations and prenatal care. Over a 10-year period, the program contributed to a 22.5% increase in girls' grade progression in rural areas and an 18% increase in urban areas.[68]
- In Bangladesh, Pakistan, and Turkey, CCTs helped increase girls' enrollment in school.[69]

### 4. Hire more women teachers at every level.

In many countries, a lack of women teachers translates to fewer girls in school, as some families prefer that once their daughters reach puberty they be taught by a woman. Scarcity of women teachers is most acute in Sub-Saharan Africa.[70]

### 5. Focus on: Hygiene + Sports + GBV

Here are three more strategies that have, over time, proven effective to increase the number of girls in school and to keep girls in school.

- **Ensure that girls are healthy and have access to hygiene products.**
  Girls who have access to proper nutrition and healthcare are more likely to attend school and more able to learn when they are there.[71] For example, in Kenya, a school-based deworming program improved school performance and future earnings for girls, and increased their chances of passing the secondary-school entrance exam by 25%.[72]

  A recent analysis of 32 African countries found that enrollment of girls in school increased by 28% (compared to a 22% increase for boys) when school meal programs were offered.[73] While sex-disaggregated data isn't widely available, the impact of poor nutrition on education outcomes in the U.S. is pronounced. Many low-income children depend on school meals. During crises such as the COVID-19 pandemic this nutrition isn't as readily available, causing short-term effects such as fatigue and reduced immune response, increasing the risk of contracting communicable diseases, and leading to long-term developmental, psychological, physical, and emotional harms.[74]

  Across the globe, if a girl is menstruating and she knows there aren't sufficient hygiene products at school, she is apt to stay home, miss class, and fall behind her peers.[75] A recent World Health Organization report underscores that girls are more likely to attend school and complete their education if safe hygiene and sanitation facilities exist in schools.[76]

- **Encourage girls to play sports.**
  As we see from the intense excitement about women's sports, playing sports is transformative. Women who play sports have higher levels of confidence and self-esteem, are more likely to get good grades in school, more likely to graduate, and less likely to have an unplanned pregnancy than girls who do not play sports.[77] Playing sports helps girls and young women learn about teamwork and goal setting, behaviors critical for success in the workplace.[78] In fact, 80% of women executives at Fortune 500 companies have been active in sports.[79]

  Demand from young women for competitive sports is growing. Due to the "unprecedented" demand for women's flag football, in 2020 the National Association of Intercollegiate Athletics, the National Football League, and Reigning Champs Experiences announced it will bring this sport to college campuses as a varsity sport, with at least 15 schools committed to adding the sport to their athletics department.[80]

Olympian Lorrie Fair conducts a training session with young women in Kabul, Afghanistan.

When I interviewed Olympian Lorrie Fair, she said it well: "Sports are a part of education, and they provide both girls and boys with the opportunity to develop skills that are important in life. Aside from the obvious physical skills developed from participation in sport, children also learn skills such as team work, leadership, overcoming adversity, being a humble winner and a gracious loser.

"Studies show that when young women and girls participate in sports they are more likely to stay in school, which may have an ultimate impact on their ability to be employed and be self-sufficient. Sports are about more than the game being played."[81] Athletes like Lorrie Fair, and so many others, are role models for how sports can transform the lives of women and girls.

- **Address gender-based violence (GBV) and bullying that occurs at school.** This topic will be covered in detail in Chapter 4, but it's important to mention here. Approximately 15 million adolescent girls will experience or have experienced forced sex in their lifetime.[82] Girls are often coerced by male teachers to exchange sex for grades, or to cover school-related fees and/or costs.[83] Further, girls are much more likely than boys to be bullied at school, and are twice as likely to be cyberbullied.[84] Students who are bullied earn lower test results.[85]

Teacher with young women students building a robotic vehicle.

## ROLE MODELS AND TRAILBLAZERS

Here in the U.S. and elsewhere it is important to recognize the importance of teachers as role models. From the earliest age, boys and girls need to be exposed to both male and female teachers. Exposing them to only women teachers in elementary school reinforces the societal messaging that teaching – and caregiving – is a woman's responsibility. Further, when more women teach math and science in middle and high school, more girls are likely to study these subjects in college.[86] Boys, by contrast, are unaffected by the gender mix of their high school teachers.[87]

Credit: ©Nobel Media. Photo: Ken Opprann

In 2014, Malala Yousafzai shared the Nobel Peace Prize with Indian children's rights activist Kailash Satyarthi. At age 17, Yousafzai became the youngest person ever to receive this prize.

**Malala Yousafzai** is a global advocate for girls' education. She was born in the Swat District of Pakistan, where her father was a school owner and was active in educational issues. After Yousafzai blogged for the BBC about her experiences during the Taliban's growing influence in the region, the Taliban attempted to assassinate her on the bus home from school. She now lives in the U.K., where she just graduated from Oxford. In 2014 she shared the Nobel Peace Prize.[88]

## CONCLUSION

Making sure that girls and women have access to education is a crucial first step toward gender equality. As we've seen, education has a tremendous impact on a woman, her current and future family, her life choices, and her community. With the knowledge and skills, the self-confidence and expanded horizons that she gains from even a few years of schooling, a woman is much better equipped to effectively navigate her way through life. By advocating for reduced barriers that keep even one girl from receiving a quality education, or by doing what you can do to make it easier for her to stay in school and complete her education, you will positively impact her life and the lives of countless others.

As we move in the next chapters to consider advocacy around ensuring that women have equal access to jobs, services, health and safety, and community engagement, you will broaden your understanding of the importance of investing in girls and young women from their earliest years. Without the foundation of education, it is almost impossible for women and girls to develop their full potential and build a better world.

# HIRE MORE WOMEN IN TECH

We must increase the number of women – across the globe – who design products and technology. Cell phones are designed to fit in a man's palm. For decades, cars were designed for the average man, who was both taller and heavier than the average woman. As a result, women were 47% more likely to be injured and 17% more likely to die in a car accident than men.[89]

Most **artificial intelligence (AI)**, and the programs that utilize AI, are created by (White) men. Those programs and apps will be different than those created by a more diverse group of programmers. For example, a recent article documented that "smart speakers" such as Alexa and Home have a hard time understanding commands by those who speak English with an accent.[90]

Many U.S. universities are working to increase the number of women who graduate with **engineering degrees**, and that needs to continue.[91] According to a 2015 study, women earned over 40% of engineering degrees at top-ranked schools.[92] At Harvey Mudd College, for example, the percentage of women graduating with degrees in computer science increased from 12% to approximately 40% in five years when Harvey Mudd revised its introductory computing curricula, provided research opportunities for undergraduates after freshman year, and exposed young women students to networking opportunities.[93]

**STEM (and STEAM*) camps** help young people and teens of all skill levels discover coding, AI, machine learning, film, robotics, and game design. The U.S. Department of State, in partnership with private sector partners, conducts an annual two-week **Women in Science (WiSci) summer camp** that brings together girls from around the world for an intensive program. It is based on the premise that the most effective problem solving takes place when diverse voices and viewpoints, as well as people with different types of expertise, are involved. WiSci has been in existence since 2015, and to date has convened camps in Rwanda, Peru, Malawi, Namibia, Estonia, Kosovo, Morocco, and Indonesia.[94]
girlup.org/programs/wisci

*STEAM = STEM + art

# RESOURCES: Education
## Information Is Power

In every chapter of this book you will find a list of resources that you can refer to when you are formulating your initial questions, doing your research, finding out who has the power to make change, and making an advocacy plan. Here you will find resources to help you work to ensure that girls everywhere start school and complete their education.

These lists are available/updated at: stepheniefoster.com

## Movies and TV

- **Girl Rising (2013)** Girl Rising travels the globe to meet nine girls, striving beyond circumstance and overcoming nearly insurmountable odds to achieve their dreams. It is written by women, and voiced by Meryl Streep, Kerry Washington, and Anne Hathaway.

- **He Named Me Malala (2015)** Documentary about Nobel Peace Prize laureate Malala Yousafzai, her father's ownership of schools and activism, the rise and fall of the Tehrik-i-Taliban Pakistan in Swat Valley and the assassination attempt made against Yousafzai when she was aged 15.

- **Persepolis (2007)** The autobiographical story of a young woman who defies Islamic fundamentalists.

- **Queen of Katwe (2016)** The story of a Ugandan girl's path to becoming a chess champion.

- **The Road to Teach (2015)** The film follows three young aspiring teachers as they embark on a cross-country road trip to learn about the state of education in America. Along the way they interview current teachers about the challenges and rewards of the profession and talk about their career choices. Includes a Q&A with then-Secretary of Education Arne Duncan.

- **Selma (2014)** Based on the events of March of 1965, when civil rights demonstrators marched across an Alabama bridge and into a new era for Black Americans. Starring Carmen Ejogo, Tessa Thompson, and Lorraine Toussaint. Directed by Ava DuVernay, a Black woman director, and co-produced by Oprah Winfrey.

- **Winners of Greater Good's Girls' Voices for Change Contest** An annual contest of short films made by girls that feature creativity, resilience, and leadership in girls worldwide through the power of digital media storytelling and education.[95]

## Books

- *A Heritage of Her Own* (1979) by Nancy F. Cott. An in-depth exploration of the day-to-day lives, aspirations, accomplishments, and social relationships of women from the 17th century to the present.

- *A Woman's Crusade: Alice Paul and the Battle for Suffrage* (2010) by Mary

Walton. In 1907, Paul went to England to attend university, where she developed a passionate devotion to the suffrage movement. Upon her return to the U.S., she became the leader of the militant wing of the American suffrage movement.

- *Educated, A Memoir* (**2018**) by Tara Westover. A memoir recounting the author overcoming her survivalist Mormon family in order to go to college, and emphasizing the importance of education to enlarging her world.

- *The Glass Universe* (**2006**) by Dava Sobel. The hidden history of the women whose contributions to the burgeoning field of astronomy changed our understanding of the stars and our place in the universe.

- *I Am Malala* (**2013**) by Malala Yousafzai. Details the early life of Yousafzai, a young activist for girls' education, her father's ownership of schools and his activism, the rise and fall of the Tehrik-i-Taliban Pakistan in Swat Valley, and the assassination attempt made against Yousafzai when she was aged 15. The book has been banned in many schools in Pakistan.

- *Raise Your Hand* (**2019**) by Alice Paul Tapper, daughter of CNN's Jake Tapper. Eleven-year-old Tapper challenges girls everywhere to speak up. When she noticed that the girls in her class were not participating as much as the boys, she knew she had to do something about it.

- *Reading Lolita in Tehran* (**2003**) by Azar Nafisi. A memoir about returning to Iran during the revolution. It narrates her teaching at the University of Tehran, her refusal to wear the veil and subsequent expulsion from the university, the formation of her book club, and her decision to emigrate. Events are interlaced with stories of book club members who met weekly to discuss Western literature.

- *Speak* (**1999**) by Laurie Halse Anderson. A young-adult novel about high school freshman Melinda Sordino, who was ostracized for calling the police to break up a party where a sexual assault occurred.

- *Sold* (**2006**) by Patricia McCormick. The story of a girl from Nepal who is sold into sexual slavery in India. The novel is written in a series of short, vignette-style chapters, from the point of view of the main character, Lakshmi.

- *What Works in Girls' Education: Evidence for the World's Best Investment* (**2015**) by Gene B. Sperling and Rebecca Winthrop. Evidence on why the returns from investing in girls are so high that no nation or family can afford not to educate their girls. *What Works* is a compelling work for citizens, academics, experts, policymakers, or journalists interested in girls' education.

## Organizations

- **Aide-et-Action**
Aide-et-Action is an international NGO network working to advance the cause of development through education. The group fights for access for all to a quality education, from early childhood to adulthood. Currently, projects

are focused in Africa, France, South Asia, Southeast Asia, and China. www.aide-et-action.org

- **The Bill and Melinda Gates Foundation**
  The Gates Foundation focuses on the issues of extreme poverty in developing countries and education in the United States. Its goal is to increase the number of Black, Latinx, and low-income students who graduate through their direct grants to schools and school support organizations, training for new teachers, and expanding high quality public charter schools. www.gatesfoundation.org

- **Black Girls Code**
  The organization's goal is to increase the number of women of color in the digital space by empowering girls of color ages 7 to 17 to become innovators in STEM fields, leaders in their communities, and builders of their own futures through exposure to computer science and technology. www.blackgirlscode.com

- **CAMFED: Campaign for Female Education**
  Founded in 1993 to help a group of 32 attend secondary school, CAMFED is now a pan-African, non-governmental nonprofit that has helped more than 4.1 million children through a network of partner schools. The goal is to eradicate poverty in Africa through education of girls and empowerment of young women. www.camfed.org

- **Echidna Giving**
  Echidna is a private funder granting $500 to $700 million over the next 40 years with the sole aim of delivering the promise of girls' education. Echidna focuses on grants to support girls in early childhood and adolescence in lower-income countries. www.echidnagiving.org

- **Girl Rising**
  Girl Rising's mission is to ensure that girls around the world are educated and empowered. Girl Rising's work focuses on storytelling through film, television, social media videos, graphic novels, radio, curricula, and more in order to serve as a transformational catalyst for long-term social change and impact. The organization began with a film about nine unforgettable girls, written by award-winning authors, voiced by some of Hollywood's biggest celebrities, and translated into over 30 languages. www.girlrising.org

- **Girls Inc.**
  Girls Inc. is a network of local non-profit organizations serving girls ages 6-18 in 350 cities across the United States and Canada. Through advocacy, Girls Inc. tackles systemic barriers affecting how girls are growing up, giving girls the knowledge, resources, and skills to live healthy lives with meaningful educational opportunities. www.girlsinc.org

- **The Girl Scouts**
  With more than 1.7 million girls and 750,000 adults, the Girl Scouts is a global girls' leadership development organization. Its Public Policy and Advocacy Office works with state and national leaders to raise awareness of

issues important to girls and young women. www.girlscouts.org

- **Girls Opportunity Alliance**
  Part of the Obama Foundation, the Girls Opportunity Alliance brings together grassroots leaders supporting adolescent girls' education and works with GoFundMe to directly support these leaders. www.obama.org

- **Girls Who Code**
  Girls Who Code aims to close the gender gap in technology and STEAM. The organization provides summer and after-school programs for teen girls to learn to code. So far, over 300,000 girls have been served through in-person camps and classes. www.girlswhocode.com

- **The Global Campaign for Education (GCE)**
  Founded in 1999, The Global Campaign for Education aims to end exclusion in education, advocating at the international, national, and regional level to pressure governments and the international community to deliver everyone a free, quality education. Currently, the GCE represents over 100 international, national, and regional coalitions. www.campaignforeducation.org

- **The Global Partnership for Education**
  The Global Partnership works with over 70 partners in developing countries to help the most vulnerable children receive a quality education. It provides both technical assistance and direct funding to governments. www.globalpartnership.org

- **The Malala Fund**
  The Malala Fund was started by Malala and Ziauddin Yousafzai to help ensure a more equal world by supporting every girl's right to a free, safe, and equal education. The Fund advocates at local, national, and international levels for resources and policies to guarantee all girls have a secondary education. www.malala.org

- **Radical Monarchs**
  A scouting organization, the Radical Monarchs create opportunities for young girls of color to form fierce sisterhood, celebrate their identities, and contribute radically to their communities. Each Badge Unit involves learning about social justice and self empowerment. Examples of Radical Badges include: Black Lives Matter, Radical Pride, Pachamama Justice, and Radical Coding. www.radicalmonarchs.org

- **Room to Read**
  Room to Read's Girls' Education Program helps girls acquire the skills and agency they need to make informed choices about their lives and realize their potential. The program offers need-based material support for school costs, local mentors, and life skills classes and workshops. www.roomtoread.org

- **UNICEF Program on Girls' Education**
  UNICEF works to remove barriers to girls' schooling and promote gender equality in education. It addresses obstacles such as distance barriers, re-entry policies for young mothers, social protection measures, and menstrual hygiene issues. www.unicef.org/education/girls-education

# Facts and Figures

- **U.S. Chamber of Commerce**[96]
  The Chamber of Commerce, and its affiliated Foundation, have numerous resources about the importance of women to economic growth. As an example, the Foundation recently released a report on the critical importance of bringing more women into STEM professions.

- **The World Bank**[97]
  The Gender Data Portal is the World Bank's comprehensive source for the latest sex-disaggregated data covering demography, education, health, access to economic opportunities, public life and decision-making, and agency. The World Bank also issues a bi-annual report, "Women, Business and the Law," [98] which compiles country-specific laws that constrain women and girls.

- **World Economic Forum (WEF)**[99]
  Since 2006, the WEF Global Gender Gap Report has analyzed the laws and policies of 153 countries and benchmarked their progress against regional and global data that measure gender parity across four dimensions, including educational attainment. It also compares the relative status of and/or access to educational opportunity for men, women, boys, and girls.

These lists are available/updated at: stepheniefoster.com

# NOTES

1   See "Convention on the Elimination of All Forms of Discrimination against Women (CEDAW)," UN Women, https://bit.ly/3nN0F7c.

2   The World Bank, "The High Cost of Not Educating Girls," The World Bank, July, 2018, https://bit.ly/3pXubZM.

3   "Women Worldwide Live Longer, Healthier Lives with Better Education, Says New UN Report," UN News, October 20, 2015, https://bit.ly/37lGyq9.

4   Baum, Sandy, "Higher Education Earnings Premium: Value, Variation, and Trends," The Urban Institute, February, 2014, https://urbn.is/2VlYFGQ.

5   Sperling, Gene and Winthrop, Rebecca, "What Works in Girls' Education," The Brookings Institution, 2016, https://brook.gs/2Vi4yoD. Depending on the level of schooling, every additional year of education increases a young woman's earning power between 20% and 90% over her lifetime.

6   "Women and Girls' Education: Facts and Figures," UNESCO, 2014, https://bit.ly/39oYgvE.

7   Duffin, Erin, "Percentage of US Population Who Have Completed High School or More 1960-2019," Statista, April 1, 2020, https://bit.ly/36qquUZ; Ryan, Camille L. and Bauman, Kurt, "Educational Attainment in the United States: 2015," US Census Bureau, March 2016, https://bit.ly/2KVVfJ5.

8   Dill, Kathryn, "More Women Pursue MBAs as Elite Schools Step up Recruiting," The Wall Street Journal, November 9, 2019, https://on.wsj.com/3fSmJdN.

9   Scott, Linda, "Student Debt Forgiveness is a Women's Issue," Gen, July 22, 2020, adapted from Scott, Linda "The Double X Economy: The Epic Potential of Women's Empowerment," Farrar, Straus, and Giroux, July, 21, 2020, https://bit.ly/3qeiPAX.

10  "The State of the World's Children, 16th annual report," UNICEF, December 11, 1995, https://uni.cf/2JvBHKU.

11  "USAID Let Girls Learn Fact Sheet," USAID, https://bit.ly/2VlNMF6.

12  "The World Bank Group (WBG) and Adolescent Girls' Education Fact Sheet," The World Bank, April 23, 2016, https://bit.ly/2JqJg5H.

13  Paquette, Danielle, "Coronavirus Dims Academic Prospects of African Girls," The Washington Post, June 14, 2020, https://wapo.st/39qNjK5; Grant, Harriet, "Many Girls Have Been Cut: How global school closures left children at risk," The Guardian, https://bit.ly/3fQsbhv.

14  Adeniran, Adedeji, "Ensuring Learning Continuity for Every African Child in the Time of COVID-19," The Brookings Institution, June 4, 2020, https://brook.gs/3ob6dIZ; "Education: from disruption to recovery," UNESCO, https://bit.ly/3qhhsl2.

15  "Malala Fund Releases Report on Girls' Education and COVID-19," Malala Fund, April 6, 2020, https://bit.ly/3mpKlJq.

16  OECD, "PISA in Focus: What Kinds of Careers Do Boys and Girls Expect for Themselves?" OECD Publishing, March, 2012, https://bit.ly/3fPoxV8.

17  OECD, "The ABC of Gender Equality in Education: Aptitude, Behaviour, Confidence," PISA, OECD Publishing, 2015, https://bit.ly/3oaMHfM.

18  Increases in education accounts for 50% of the economic growth in the 36 developed countries that are members of the Organisation for Economic Cooperation and Development Meeting of the OECD Council at Ministerial Level, https://bit.ly/2Vm3KyU. OECD countries include: Australia, Austria, Belgium, Canada, Chile, The Czech Republic, Denmark, Estonia, Finland, France, Germany, Greece, Hungary, Iceland, Ireland, Israel, Italy, Japan, Korea, Latvia, Lithuania, Luxembourg, Mexico, The Netherlands, New Zealand, Norway, Poland, Portugal, The Slovak Republic, Slovenia, Spain, Sweden, Switzerland, Turkey, the United Kingdom, and the United States of America. The OECD also found that continued and more expansive economic growth could occur as job categories are opened to women across all economic sectors, but that

educational equality alone does not guarantee economic equality as long as women c
ontinue to bear the main burden of unpaid household work.

19 Ibid.

20 Wodon, Quentin et al, "Missed Opportunities: The High Cost of Not Educating Girls," The World Bank, July, 2018, https://bit.ly/3pXubZM.

21 "Girls' Education," USAID, October 1, 2018, https://bit.ly/37r0tnP.

22 "Infographic: An Educated Girl Has a Ripple Effect, USAID," November 10, 2014, https://bit.ly/3fQkY0Z.

23 Becktold, Wendy, "Educating Girls May Be Nigeria's Best Defense Against Climate Change," Sierra, October 29, 2019, https://bit.ly/3o9nXnT.

24 "Wynes, Seth and Nicholas, Kimberly A, "The Climate Mitigation Gap: Education and government recommendations miss the most effective individual actions," IOP Science, July 12, 2017, https://bit.ly/3qiosOk.

25 Becktold, Wendy, "Educating Girls May Be Nigeria's Best Defense Against Climate Change," Sierra, October 29, 2019, https://bit.ly/3o9nXnT.

26 UNESCO, "Girls Education: The Facts," Education for All Global Monitoring Report, October, 2013, https://bit.ly/3mkhhmx.

27 Ibid.

28 Ajikobi, David, "Does Nigeria Have the World's Most Girls Out-of-School, as Activist Malala Claimed?" Africa Check, August 10, 2017, https://bit.ly/37kotZy.

29 Vohra, Parth, "Education Still Eludes Many Pakistani Girls," Voice of America News, November 20, 2017, https://bit.ly/3fQwM34.

30 Guyatt, Tanya, "Millions of Girls are Out of School, But Data Show that Gender Alone is Not the Main Culprit," UNESCO Institute of Statistics, https://bit.ly/2KP1n5D.

31 "Girls' Education," UNICEF, https://uni.cf/3qip8mT.

32 Davies, Jane, "For Girls, Conflict Can Mean the End of School," Global Partnership for Education, June 27, 2018, https://bit.ly/37ppoYz.

33 "Goal 4: Quality Education," United Nations Development Programme, https://bit.ly/33z1gSu.

34 "Two-thirds of the World's Illiterate Adults are Women, Report Finds," The Guardian, https://bit.ly/3fQC5iY.

35 Matthews, Jay, "These Top-Flight All-Girls Public Schools are Proving the Value of Single-Sex Education," The Washington Post, June 3, 2020, https://wapo.st/33wTWGL.

36 Ibid.

37 See https://www.kakenyasdream.org.

38 Ibid.

39 Ibid.

40 See, e.g., DC State Board of Education website, https://sboe.dc.gov/page/sboe-meeting-information.

41 Ozler, Berk, "What Works to Keep Adolescent Girls in School? A Three-Part Series," World Bank Blogs, September 14, 2015, https://bit.ly/2JopMyz.

42 Day, Jennifer Cheeseman, "Among the Educated, Women Earn 74 Cents for Every Dollar Men Make," US Census Bureau, College Degrees Widen Gender Earnings Gap, May 29, 2019, https://bit.ly/3ltk8rT.

43 Ozler, Berk, "What Works to Keep Adolescent Girls in School? A Three-Part Series," World Bank Blogs, September 14, 2015, https://bit.ly/2JopMyz.

44 Ibid.

45 Ibid.

46 Auxier, Brooke and Anderson, Monica, "As Schools Close Due to the Coronavirus, Some U.S. Students Face a Digital 'Homework Gap'," Pew Research Center, March 16, 2020, https://pewrsr.ch/39qcDjj.

47 Fishbane, Lara and Tomer, Adie, "As Classes Move Online During COVID-19, What are Disconnected Students to Do?" The Avenue, The Brookings Institution, March 20, 2020,

https://brook.gs/39uxmm3.

48  https://www.imdb.com/title/tt3065132/.

49  https://www.imdb.com/title/tt2444946/.

50  Alexander, Sadof, "7 Films by Girls Who Are Passionate About Education," One, January 31, 2018, https://www.one.org/us/blog/films-shorts-girls-education/.

51  Kid World Citizen, "Books About Girls in School," March 31, 2015, https://kidworld-citizen.org/books-about-girls-in-school-fighting-for-their-education/.

52  www.girlswhocode.com.

53  www.blackgirlscode.com.

54  Ruble, Diane et al, "The Role of Gender Constancy in Early Gender Development," Society for Research in Child Development, July 19, 2007, https://bit.ly/3mvvZr6.

55  Rooms, Sven and Muhwezi, Martha, "New Toolkit Empowers Teachers to Challenge Gender Stereotypes," The Brookings Institution, March 1, 2019, https://brook.gs/2JmJbA5.

56  Ibid.

57  "World Development Report: LEARNING to Realize Education's Promise," The World Bank, 2018, https://bit.ly/36mmC79; Morgan, Claire, et al, "A Systematic Review of the Evidence of the Impact of Eliminating School User Fees in Low-Income Developing Countries," London: EPPI-Centre, Social Science Research Unit, Institute of Education, University of London, 2012, https://bit.ly/3qf3m3A.

58  Duflo, Esther, Dupas, Pascaline and Kremer, Michael, "Preventing HIV and Teen Pregnancy in Kenya: The Roles of Teacher Training and Education Subsidies," *American Economic Review*, 2015, https://bit.ly/39p3KGK.

59  Alderman, Harold, "The Impact of Food for Education Programs on School Participation in Northern Uganda," *Economic Development and Cultural Change*, 61 (1) October, 2012, https://bit.ly/2VqxhHH.

60  Duflo, Esther, et al, "Returns to Secondary Schooling in Ghana," J-PAL, https://bit.ly/3qf3WOK.

61  Iversen, Katja, "For Girls, Success Starts with Safe Schools," Reuters Foundation, May 7, 2016, https://bit.ly/3mFfZm4.

62  Burde, Dana, and Leigh L. Linden, "Bringing Education to Afghan Girls: A Randomized Controlled Trial of Village-Based Schools," *American Economic Journal: Applied Economics* 5(3): 27-40, 2013, https://bit.ly/2Vpl7yY. In rural areas, 25% of children are out of school compared to 16% in urban areas.

63  United Nations Children's Fund (UNICEF), "Hidden in Plain Sight: A statistical analysis of violence against children," UNICEF, September 3, 2014, https://bit.ly/37kRBQq.

64  Trainer, Mark, "5 Ways to Keep Girls in School," Share America, March 28, 2016, https://bit.ly/36slzTy.

65  Burde, Dana, and Leigh L. Linden, "Bringing Education to Afghan Girls: A randomized controlled trial of village-based schools," *American Economic Journal: Applied Economics* 5(3): 27-40, 2013, https://bit.ly/2Vpl7yY.

66  Tabarrok, Alex, "Triple Distancing Bikes in India," Marginal Revolution, May 23, 2015, https://bit.ly/2JBuOHH.

67  Berk Ozler, "What Works to Keep Adolescent Girls in School? Part 3," The World Bank, October 25, 2015, https://bit.ly/3fXCMqX.

68  De Brauw, A, et al, "The Impact of Bolsa Família on Women's Decision-Making Power," World Development, 59, 487–504, 2014.

69  Fiszbein, Ariel; et al, "Conditional Cash Transfers: Reducing present and future poverty," World Bank Policy Research Report, 2009, https://bit.ly/3lwPJsJ.

70  Global Partnership for Education, "Educating Girls: The path to gender equality," May, 2019, https://bit.ly/36pAOMK.

71  "Girls' Education," The World Bank, September 25, 2017, https://bit.ly/2Jh56c4.

72  "Deworming to Increase School Attendance," J-PAL, https://bit.ly/2KY5Seo.

73 Borkowski, Artur et al, "With Schools Closed, Hundreds of Millions of Children are Not Receiving School Meals," Center for Global Development, March 24, 2020, https://bit.ly/3qcBY6l.

74 Caroline G. Dunn, Ph.D., R.D., et al, "Feeding Low-Income Children During the Covid-19 Pandemic," *The New England Journal of Medicine*, April 30, 2020, https://bit.ly/2JhBXxr.

75 Vashisht, Aditi, et al, "School Absenteeism During Menstruation Amongst Adolescent Girls in Delhi, India," *Journal of Family & Community Medicine*, Sep-Dec 2018; 25(3): 163–168 found at https://bit.ly/39tlsc9.

76 See Water, "Sanitation and Hygiene Standards for Schools in Low-cost Settings," World Health Organization, at https://bit.ly/33yktn0.

77 Davidson, Kavitha, "Study Shows Positive Correlation Between Playing Sports, Better Self-image Among Girls," ESPN, March 30, 2018, https://es.pn/37o9a2a.

78 "Benefits: Why Sports Participation for Girls and Women," Women's Sports Foundation, August 30, 2016, https://bit.ly/36qzGbD.

79 Zarya, Valentina, "What Do 65% of the Most Powerful Women Have in Common? Sports," *Fortune*, September 22, 2017, https://bit.ly/36s3tAN.

80 "NAIA to Sponsor Women's Flag Football with NFL Partnership," *Sports Illustrated*, May 4, 2020, https://bit.ly/37s8FDZ.

81 Stephenie Foster, "Sitting Down with Olympian Lorrie Fair; Reflections on Afghanistan," HuffPost, https://bit.ly/37tuUJM.

82 "Facts and Figures: Ending violence against women," UN Women, page last updated November, 2019, https://bit.ly/3lwSJW1.

83 Global Partnership for Education, "Educating Girls: The path to gender equality," May, 2019, https://bit.ly/36pAOMK.

84 "Girls are More Likely to be Bullied than Boys English School Survey Finds," *The Guardian*, https://bit.ly/3mrHteY.

85 Kibriya et al., "The Effects of School-Related Gender-Based Violence on Academic Performance: Evidence from Botswana, Ghana, and South Africa," USAID, 2016, https://bit.ly/3mukTCD.

86 The Hechinger Report, "Is the Teaching Profession Not Pink Enough?" *US News and World Report*, March 9, 2015, https://bit.ly/3fZcbtI.

87 Ibid.

88 The Nobel Prize, "Malala Yousafzai Facts," https://bit.ly/3mxQRhe.

89 Emma Goldberg, "A World Made for Men," *The New York Times*, 2020, https://nyti.ms/36qBkKl.

90 Drew Harwell, "The Accent Gap," *The Washington Post*, July 19, 2018, https://wapo.st/37rynsm.

91 Nick Anderson, "At Top Public Universities, a Mixed Record for Women in Engineering," *The Washington Post*, September 21, 2016, https://wapo.st/37qiHFN.

92 "Women in STEM," Best Colleges, https://bit.ly/3qfTyGt.

93 "New Report on Women in STEM Features Harvey Mudd's CS Program," Harvey Mudd College News, March 26, 2015, https://bit.ly/39xfB5B.

94 "WiSci (Women in Science) Steam Camp Partnership," US Department of State, https://bit.ly/3mvmGXX.

95 https://girlsvoices.greatergood.org/top-videos-gallery/.

96 "Reaching the Full Potential of STEM for Women and the U.S. Economy," U.S. Chamber of Commerce Foundation, https://bit.ly/2JA8OwU.

97 www.worldbank.org.

98 https://wbl.worldbank.org/#.

99 www.weforum.org.

CHAPTER THREE

# The Missing Half

*Simply put, when money flows into the hands of women who have the authority to use it, everything changes.*

Melinda French Gates

*I am not satisfied in making money for myself. I endeavor to provide employment to hundreds of women of my race.*

Madame C. J. Walker
Entrepreneur and first woman
millionaire in the U.S.

Women are critical to economic growth, but our abilities and contributions are almost always undervalued and rarely appreciated, let alone acknowledged. The systems and biases that have kept women from reaching their economic potential, individually and collectively, have been in place for a long time. COVID-19 has magnified the numerous inequalities women face at work and at home, with early data reflecting that women have lost their jobs at higher rates than men,[1] are experiencing high and sustained unemployment rates,[2] and are under more pressure to give up their jobs due to care responsibilities.[3] But, at the same time, the pandemic has inspired new ways of thinking about work and how to end these inequalities.[4]

Increasing a woman's participation in the economy is not only good for the individual woman, but it is also good for her family, for her community, and for her country. We know that if women participated in their economies at the same level as men, global GDP would increase by $12 to $28 trillion.[5] Societies with greater gender equality and economic participation by women:

- Grow faster and more equitably
- Have lower rates of poverty
- Offer a wider array of consumer choices
- More successfully encourage innovation

Investors are now focused on the need for diversity in companies, as recent studies find that companies with a more diverse workforce perform better.[6] For example, stock prices increase when companies report better-than-expected gender diversity, and they fall when firms don't do as well as expected.[7]

## WOMEN IN THE C-SUITE

Women hold only 24% of senior corporate roles in the U.S.[8]

- Only 7% of Fortune 500 CEOs are women and less than 1% are Black women.[9]

Increasing these numbers increases the bottom line.

- Companies with more women on executive committees had a 47% greater return on equity than those companies with no women on these committees.[10]
- Firms with more women senior managers recognize a financial performance benefit of up to 15%.[11]
- Companies with more women on boards have better environmental performance, being 60% more likely to reduce energy consumption.[12]

Breaking the proverbial glass ceiling:

- In September 2020, Jane Fraser was named Citibank's new CEO, and she is the first woman to ever lead a major Wall Street bank.[13]
- General Motors CEO Mary Barra, former PepsiCo CEO Indra Nooyi, and former Hewlett-Packard CEO Carly Fiorina are other examples of women who have broken this barrier – and are role models for so many.

There need to be more women like them.

In order to increase the participation of women in economies on a local and global scale we need:

- More women in the formal labor force
- More women being promoted
- More women in senior management
- More women on corporate boards
- More women starting and growing businesses
- More women speaking up at work every day
- Equal access to education and training
- A legal framework that supports women's economic opportunity
- A greater commitment by organizations in every sector to gender equality, pay equity, and non-discrimination

# LEGAL REFORMS MUST ADDRESS GENDER DIFFERENCES EMBEDDED IN LAWS

According to a 2021 World Bank report,[14] **women and men have equal legal rights in only ten countries**: Belgium, Canada, Denmark, France, Iceland, Ireland, Latvia, Luxembourg, Portugal, and Sweden. This is not enough. Laws and policies must enable and increase women's economic participation so that every woman has equal opportunity at work, whether at the executive level or in entry-level positions. Almost three billion women do not have equal access to the job market.[15] Of 190 economies assessed in the World Bank report, 88 have laws preventing women from working in specific jobs, many do not prohibit sexual harassment in the workplace, and in at least 15 economies, husbands can legally prevent their wives from working.[16]

Further, the 2021 report highlights how governments have addressed the impact of COVID-19 on women. Before the pandemic, less than 25% of economies guaranteed parents any time off for childcare; since the pandemic, 40 more economies have enacted policies to help parents with childcare. In addition, governments introduced about 120 new measures such as hotlines and shelters to protect women from the increase in gender-based violence that has occurred during COVID, as well as allowing remote court proceedings for family matters.[17]

We need to abolish laws that constrain a woman's ability to make economic decisions that maximize her skills and abilities. Incentives to bring women into the formal economy include passing and enforcing equal-pay laws and anti-discrimination laws, creating family-leave policies, and mandating equal access to all job categories.

There has been progress, but we still need to push harder. Over the past decade, 131 economies have changed 274 laws to increase gender equality in the worplace.[18] This includes 35 economies that passed laws prohibiting workplace sexual harassment, protecting nearly two billion more women.[19] In the last year alone, 27 economies have reformed 45 discriminatory laws.[20]

As we confront the COVID-19 pandemic, these legal reforms are even more critical because, despite progress made, 80% of single-parent families in the U.S. are headed by women, and nearly a third of those families live in poverty.[21] Women are the majority of minimum-wage workers in the U.S.,[22] and many have either lost their jobs as their employers scale back or close, or they are working without adequate paid sick leave in retail or other essential businesses.

## ADDRESSING GENDER PAY GAPS

In addition to tearing down legal barriers to job access, we must address gender pay gaps. Globally, women earn 77% of what men earn,[23] and lower wages mean less money for day-to-day needs, savings, emergencies, and retirement. This data understates the real extent of gender pay gaps, particularly since many women are either self-employed or work in the informal sector.

In the U.S.:

- Women earn 80% of what White men earn
- Black women earn 66% of what White men earn
- Hispanic women earn 60% of what White men earn[24]

According to the Institute for Women's Policy Research, if current trends continue, it will take:

- 39 years for this gap to close completely for White women (by 2056)
- 107 years for Black women (by 2124)
- 231 years for Hispanic women (by 2248)[25]

This data translates into very real economic consequences. Over a 40-year career, the average Black woman earns almost a million dollars ($946,120) less than a White man, and must work 18 months to make what a White man makes in 12 months.[26] According to the National Women's Law Center, a Black woman in Washington, D.C., loses $2 million over her lifetime because of the wage gap, and would need to work to the age of 98 to make what a White man makes by age 60.[27]

One way to measure this pay gap is "Equal Pay Day." March 24, 2021, was the date on which – when combining her 2021 earnings up to March 24 and her entire 2020 earnings – the typical woman made the same amount that a typical man earned in 2020 alone. The key phrase in that sentence is "typical woman." Equal Pay Day comes much later in the year for Black and Hispanic women.[28]

The pay gap also has a negative impact on retirement, as women receive only 70% of what men receive in retirement income, due to the fact that women's pensions or Social Security benefits are calculated on lower contributions and pay.[29]

## IS THERE A PAY GAP WHERE YOU WORK?

Ask if there is a pay gap between men and women holding the same or similar positions in your company or organization, and whether your organization has performed a pay study. As noted, globally, women are paid less than men.[30] In the U.S., according to *Time* magazine, a typical woman will earn at least $590,000 less than a man over the course of her lifetime.[31] These pay gaps can't be addressed unless a company or organization uncovers the gap and changes its policies.

### The Gender Pay Gap Exists Across the Globe

In the European Union, the gender pay gap is 16% and hasn't budged over the last 10 years.[32] It is widening in places like China,[33] signaling a dramatic and downward shift in women's economic opportunity. In 1990, Chinese women earned 80% of what their male counterparts earned, but today, urban Chinese women earn 67% of what men earn, and rural Chinese women earn only 56%.[34] At the same time, labor-force participation rates for Chinese women have plummeted in the last 30 years from 75% to 61%.[35]

To promote women's ability to provide for themselves and their families around the world, we need to make sure that women have equal:

- Access to capital and credit
- Property rights
- Access to influential business networks
- Access to appropriate training and knowledge of the right skills for their businesses to compete and grow

- Access to needed support services including more flexible work schedules and child care

Paid leave is especially important, as it improves the health of women and children, boosts men's participation in caregiving, and helps retain women in the workforce.[36]

# ADVOCACY AND ACTION: WHAT'S THE FIRST STEP?

In Chapter One, I identified the **Framework for Advocacy and Action**. Let's use that framework in terms of advocacy and organizing for increased access to economic opportunity for women.

### 1. Identify An Issue You Care About

The general focus for this chapter is ensuring that women have equal economic opportunity. You can narrow this to focus, for instance, on ensuring that women-owned businesses can easily borrow needed capital, or that companies and governments use their buying power to purchase (or procure) goods and services from women-owned or managed companies. Narrowing your focus sharpens your goals and makes the rest of the work easier to accomplish and act upon.

### 2. Research: Do Current Laws or Programs Disadvantage Women?

Once you have a focus, then find out if there are laws or policies that impede the ability of women-owned businesses to borrow money or get credit. **Are there laws or bank policies that make that harder?** This can take the form of policies that discriminate against women-owned or smaller businesses, capitalization or credit requirements that are onerous, or practices that favor businesses owned by men or by friends of those making decisions about loans and credit.

### 3. Investigate the Context So You Can Understand the Landscape

While every country is different, we know that increasing women's economic engagement drives growth and prosperity and gives women more control over their own lives. Laws and policies that can impede women's ability to participate in the economy include:

- Discriminatory laws about what jobs women can hold
- Policies that create and perpetuate gender pay gaps
- Policies that restrict access to credit
- Laws that don't allow women to own and have legal title to property, which can be used both as a productive asset and also as collateral for credit
- Lack of access to networks that provide information about opportunities

Once you have a focus, then find out which of the issues outlined above (or another issue) is most important to you in terms of ensuring access to economic opportunity for women, so you know what needs to be addressed through advocacy.

### 4. Find Out Who Has the Power to Make Change

Let's say you want to focus on the laws and policies that make it difficult for women-owned and managed businesses to borrow the money needed to start and grow. **Create a power map** (see Chapter 1, Step 4). This will help you figure out who has power to deal with this issue. There are many people and institutions that will have an impact. You could focus on local, state, or federal policymakers if there are legal barriers to address and laws to change. You could focus on individual banks (and bankers) or organizations that represent financial services companies, which can set policies. In all likelihood, it's a combination of these people and institutions.

## 5. Define Your Interest in This Issue

Once you have identified your issue, and know who has the power to make the necessary changes, it is important to communicate to the person you will be talking to **why this issue is important enough to trigger your actions**. This is a critical step. You will need to decide how to approach this issue and clarify your focus.

If your advocacy work is about laws and policies that make it hard for women-owned businesses to borrow money, you will need to use your research from Step 2 to identify: 1) any legal barriers to these businesses borrowing money, 2) the banks or other financial institutions that are identified as problems, and 3) what specific changes you would make to the bank's policies (see Step 7, below). It is also important to identify women who have had difficulty obtaining loans.

If you are one of the women who has faced this issue, tell your story. If you aren't personally affected, find and identify others who are so they can tell their stories. You could identify several women business owners as well as organizations that work with women business owners, such as local women's chambers of commerce, to reinforce the scope of the problem and its impact. It is also good to identify banks or financial institutions that get it right, so you can point to them as positive examples and role models. Be clear, concise/short, concrete/understandable and convincing. (See Chapter 1, Step 5.) Then put together a short summary of what you want to accomplish, your reasoning, and the impact of this change.

## 6. Prepare Your Questions

Before you ask the powers-that-be questions about how to make it easier for women-owned businesses to get credit, be prepared to make the case that increasing women's ability to start and grow business leads to economic growth and prosperity.

- Use the research that demonstrates that globally **if women participated in their economies at the same level as men, GDP would increase by $12 to $28 trillion.**[37]
- Reinforce the importance of addressing COVID's differential economic impact on women and regressive effect on gender equality. According to McKinsey & Company,[38] women make up 39% of global employment but account for 54% of overall job losses, due in large part to the increased burden of unpaid care, which is disproportionately carried by women. If no action is taken to counter these effects, McKinsey estimates that global GDP growth could be $1 trillion lower in 2030 than it would be if women's unemployment simply tracked that of men.[39] Conversely, taking action to advance gender equality could add $13 trillion to global GDP in 2030 compared with the gender-regressive scenario.[40]
- Review the information in **Diving Deep** (below).
- Review the material suggested in the **Resources** section of this chapter. (remember: INFORMATION IS POWER!).

Here are some specific questions to ask **bankers**:

- Is there a law regarding non-discrimination in terms of loans? What is it?
- What is your written policy regarding loans?
- How many loans (over the last year, the past 5 years) have you made to:
  - businesses owned by men?
  - businesses owned by women?
- Why is there a discrepancy?
- What are the reasons that you don't loan funds to women-owned businesses in the same proportion as to businesses owned by men?

Here are some specific questions to ask **business leaders and executives**. You may not know any business executives personally, but you can engage with companies and their leadership on social media, through blogs and op-eds, and by raising issues as an advocate.

- How many members of your company's Board of Directors are women and people of color? (What percentage of the board do they comprise?)
- How many members of your senior management team are women and people of color? (What percentage of senior management do they comprise?)
- Who are the highest-ranking women in your company?
- What are your company's written policies on hiring and promotion?
- How does your company track pay to ensure there aren't gender or racial disparities?
- Have you made public commitments to diversity? What are they?
- Has your company signed onto the United Nations Women's Empowerment Principles (WEPs)? (See more on WEPs in **Diving Deep**.)
- Is your company EDGE certified? (See more on EDGE Certification in **Diving Deep**.)
- How do you ensure that you don't use forced labor?
- How do you monitor compliance with these policies?
- How is this information accessible to the public?

### 7. Develop Suggestions for Solving the Challenges You Are Raising

It's important to suggest solutions for the issue you are raising. If you don't, those with power may dismiss you and question your commitment. **The solution you propose doesn't have to be perfect, or solve the entire problem.** But putting *something* forward reflects your seriousness and interest in making change. It also gives your effort more focus, which makes it easier for others to organize around it and thus amplify your message. Here are some ideas to get you going:

- If you want to address pay gaps, suggest a pay study across your organization, as described above. Make sure that the study is done in every location – both in the U.S. and abroad – and at every level. Organize others to also make the case at the leadership level. Underscore that this is good for every employee, and that in some cases men's salaries will be increased, as they were at Salesforce.[41]
- If you want to increase the amount your organization procures from women-

owned businesses, advocate for targets for that purchasing, such as setting a goal of purchasing 35% of goods and services from certified women-owned businesses. If your organization is serious about reaching this goal, it is important that it develop a way to track that spending.

## 8. Ask Your Questions and Outline Your Suggestions

There are many ways to ask the questions you've developed, and you should use the combination that works for you. You can:

- Make an appointment to ask your questions. Bring women who have been adversely affected by the policy or law.
- Send a letter or email.
- Engage on social media about your issue with others who share your views, or with decision-makers.
- Ask in person at meetings or if you see the policy maker in person at an event.
- Make an appointment specifically to talk about the issue, ask your questions, and if appropriate be ready with a concrete ask for the meeting. For example, you can ask the person you are meeting with if they will consider a policy change or sponsor relevant legislation (if needed), or ask if they will commit to looking into the issue and consider your suggestion for action on the issue. **Or at the very least, ask them if you can meet again in a month to discuss progress.**

If you need a script for your conversation, here's a start. You should only address one issue in each phone call, video chat, or letter:

> *Hello, my name is _____, and I am a constituent of President/Governor/Senator _____. I am calling/writing to urge that Senator ___ vote yes (or no) on bill number ___, about women's access to credit. Do you know how she will vote?*

Asking questions forces these institutions to gather data in order to answer you. Absent a question, people may not know that their bank's policies and practices are discriminatory. A credit union may know the number of women-owned businesses that receive loans, but may not keep track of how many women-owned businesses receive loans (or are turned down) in comparison to businesses owned by men. An organization may have never looked at the impact of its purchasing decisions.

Making a suggestion demonstrates your commitment to the issue and, if you've done your homework, the person you are meeting with will at least consider following through on your ideas *in some way*, or will open up a dialogue about how to move forward in another way.

## 9. What's Next? Follow up!

Once you have taken all of these steps, keep the pressure on decision-makers so that your issue isn't forgotten. In other words, **following up is important**. This means:

- **MOST IMPORTANT:** Send a thank-you note. In most cases you will want to include a recap of what was discussed.
- Consider working with an "organizing and advocacy partner." This can be a friend or family member who can serve as a sounding board and a collaborator as you strategize and move forward.
- More than likely there will be a number of actions you can take after your

initial meeting. Work with your advocacy partner or with the organization you are working with on the issue to come up with a plan of action.

- Ask for another meeting (remember to get to know the staff who support the decision-maker as they can be helpful in setting up that next meeting).
- Monitor the issue and your progress.
- Identify and engage with other individuals who are interested in the issue. Start to organize them to take action.
- Identify and engage with those who can influence the relevant decision-makers on your issue.
- Develop a tracking system if you are trying to get legislation introduced or a policy changed. Include names and pertinent information on:
  - Legislators who are co-sponsors
  - Decision-makers who can change policy
  - Legislators who (and how many) support you
  - Legislators who (and how many) oppose you (this last item is particularly important!).
- Develop an easy way to report to others interested in increasing women's access to economic opportunity, particularly access to credit, about your progress via email, social media, and/or a public website.

## TAKE ACTION IN YOUR DAILY LIFE!

You may decide that the most important thing you can do is **raise awareness at home**. If that is the case, then engage people at the grassroots and make the case that people in your community should care **about helping women participate more fully in the economy**.

### 1. Buy from women-owned businesses.

Every day we spend money on goods and services, whether for ourselves, our family and friends, or as part of our jobs. This gives each of us multiple opportunities to use our spending power to benefit women. Make a conscious commitment to look for companies owned and/or managed by women. If you own or manage a business, commit to purchasing as many of your goods and services from women-owned or women-managed businesses as possible, and ask your employees to always consider buying from women-owned businesses.

Buying from women-owned businesses is important at every level. The 224 million women entrepreneurs globally represent 35% of firms in the formal economy.[42] Despite this, less than 1% of corporate or government purchasing is from women-owned businesses.[43] Increasing this percentage of spend will have a tremendous impact.

Such spending can include everything from IT, catering, and accounting services to clothing, jewelry, food, and gifts. **Janet's List** is a website that maintains a list of businesses in the U.K. owned by Black women and women of color.[44] The **Women Owned**[45] directory lists women-owned businesses in the U.S. and abroad. The businesses in **Women Owned** are certified by one of two entities: the Women's Business Enterprise National Council and WEConnect International. Being certified means that the business is at least 51% owned, operated, controlled, and managed by a woman or women. **Minerva** is another directory.[46] In addition to directories, you can also:

- Ask vendors you currently use, and stores you visit, if they are women-owned or managed.
- Create your own list of businesses that are women-owned and/or managed, and share that information with your friends, family, and neighbors.
- If they don't already, ask businesses that are women-owned to note that on their websites and in advertisements.

## 2. Use your networks of friends and co-workers to support other women.

All of us have networks, starting with people we meet in our neighborhood, at school or work, during community activities, or through shared interests. We are sometimes hesitant to use these networks for business development. But being an active part of a network can increase your economic options and opportunity as well as open up economic opportunity for other women. Networks are a good source of new customers. Networks allow women to come together to identify common challenges and to brainstorm about how to solve problems and move forward. Networks help women gain the information and skills necessary to be successful in our jobs and careers, or to pivot to something new.

## 3. Suggest a woman when you are asked for an idea about whom to hire, or when you are asked to recommend a speaker.

Being asked for recommendations is a compliment, not a burden. Use it as an opportunity to promote women's expertise and skills. Be thoughtful, and suggest one or two women in your broader network. If you fit the bill, put your own name forward. That isn't arrogant. It is about knowing your worth and acknowledging your own expertise. You can also use databases – such as **Women Also Know Stuff**,[47] or **The Women Experts' Network**[48] – to identify women experts. While you are on those sites, remember to register as an expert so others can find and recommend *you*.

## 4. Encourage and promote the careers of other women – be a sponsor rather than a mentor!

Many of you have mentors or are mentors to others. But most women are actually over-mentored and under-sponsored.[49] A sponsor is more powerful, and has a larger impact on career advancement. In a nutshell, a mentor advises you face-to-face, a sponsor advocates for you when you're not in the room (e.g., when senior leadership discusses assignments and promotions). This is how senior male executives have historically promoted talented younger male colleagues. Other differences are: [50]

- **Mentors discuss** how to build skills, qualities, and confidence for career advancement with mentees. **Sponsors promote** their protégés, using their networks to connect them to higher-profile assignments and people.
- **Mentors help craft** a career vision. **Sponsors help drive** those visions.
- **Mentors share the "unwritten rules"** for advancement in their organization with mentees. **Sponsors actively involve** protégés in order to enable advancement.

Recent research by PayScale[51] indicates that having a sponsor leads to increased pay.

Employees with a White, male sponsor received pay increases more often.[52] Most employees with a White, male sponsor were also White men, while only 60% of Black and Hispanic women had a White sponsor.[53] Black and Hispanic women with a sponsor of the same race or ethnicity made, respectively, 11% and 16% less than if they had a White sponsor.[54]

**5. Ask your employer to sign the No-manels Pledge.** (no male-only panels)

This pledge increases opportunities for women to become more visible.[55] In 2018, men made up 68% of the speakers at conferences, trade shows, marketing events, and other gatherings, a small improvement from 2016 when 70% of the speakers at these gatherings were men.[56] Manels make it harder for women – at every level – to showcase what they know. Advocate for your own organization to sign the pledge so that no speakers from your organization appear on manels.

**6. Encourage the men in your life to share the burden of unpaid care and domestic work.**

Unpaid household work is critical to how we function as a society, but we still don't recognize its value or see it as "real" work. **Women perform at least two-and-a-half times more unpaid household and care-giving work than men.**[57] Even when both parents work full-time, women are responsible for the majority of child care and housework. Women spend twice as much time as men on house cleaning and preparing food, three times as much time on laundry, and almost four times as much on child care.[58] This has an impact on women's ability to work outside the home, to work the extra hours sometimes needed for career advancement, or to engage in political and civic activities.

COVID-19 has laid bare the reality that most care-giving is still done by women and is still unpaid. The closing of schools and daycare centers pushed care work back into the home, alongside paid work being done there as well. This situation has been magnified now that women are working at home and still responsible for most or all household and care-giving responsibilities.[59] With schools closed there is the added burden of home-schooling, a set of tasks shouldered largely by women.[60]

According to a recent *New York Times* report, if American women earned minimum wage for their unpaid work, collectively their wages would amount to $1.5 trillion a year.[61] Globally, the unpaid work women do caring for others represents

## NOT ALL ROLE MODELS ARE WOMEN

National Basketball Association (NBA) star LeBron James stunned many when he decided to leave the Miami Heat and return to his hometown to play with the Cleveland Cavaliers. Though he is not technically a full-time dad, his three kids were the reason.

"I started thinking about what it would be like to raise my family in my hometown," he wrote in a letter that explained his return to the place where he grew up. "I looked at other teams, but I wasn't going to leave Miami for anywhere except Cleveland. The more time passed, the more it felt right. This is what makes me happy."[64]

$10.9 trillion, if it were paid at the minimum wage.[62] This translates to between 10% and almost 40% of a country's GDP, which represents a **greater contribution to the economy than the manufacturing, commerce, or transportation sectors.**[64]

**7. Ask what type of hiring practices your organization uses.** In order to break old-fashioned hiring cycles, an organization's application process needs to be gender-blind, NOT gender-neutral. Recent research in the *Harvard Business Review* finds that removing "gendered" names (called "anonymizing") from resumes increased the number of women hired in scientific research positions.[65] Another study indicates that when salary history information in job interviews is not required, pay levels for women and Blacks increase by at least 5%.[66]

A recent study found that by just adding six words to job descriptions – part-time, full-time, job share or flexible working – applications from women for management roles at the U.K. insurance company Zurich jumped 20%.[67]

## ANONYMIZING WORKS

One of the most well-known examples of anonymizing has to do with orchestra auditions. When U.S. orchestras required musicians to audition from behind a screen, the likelihood of selecting women increased by 30%, and by the 1990s, there was a 25% increase overall in women's representation in orchestras.[68]

When the COVID pandemic made oral entrance exams impossible, women's admission rates to the literature program at a prestigious French postgraduate school jumped 16% when based entirely on a blind, written test.[69]

Ask how your organization handles other "identity cues," such as where the person lives or went to school, the applicant's extracurricular activities, as well as the language that the job seeker uses to describe their accomplishments. It's important to "muffle" those details so they do not influence hiring decisions.[70]

**8. Consider supporting startups or businesses founded by women if you have any money to invest.** Startups founded by women are 20% more likely to generate revenue, and have a 35% higher return on investment than those founded by men.[71] Founding teams that include a woman outperform their all-male peers by 63%.[72] In 2017, however, only 2% of venture funding went to women-led startups.[48]

More funders are investing in companies led by diverse founders, but progress is slow. Here are some examples of new ways to think about investing:

- In 2019, the Operator Collective launched a $45 million fund. The investors (limited partners) were 90% women, 40% people of color, and 77% new to tech investment. Two important points: Most investors had never been asked to invest in a fund before and, second, there was a sliding scale for investment, with some investors starting at the $10,000 level.[74]
- In 2019, Backstage Capital announced a $36 million fund investing exclusively in companies led by Black women founders. Sarah Kunst, a Black angel-fund investor and entrepreneur, recently closed a $3.5 million venture capital fund, called Cleo Capital, to make women a larger part of the decision-making

process in venture capital.[75]

- Next Wave Impact Fund was founded in 2015 to increase diversity, inclusion, and impact in early-stage investing. Its current global fund has 99 women investors – 25 of them women of color – and a portfolio of 15 companies, diversified across industry and geography. All of the companies in the portfolio are led by women and people of color.[77]

## SUMMARY

This chapter outlines how limits on women's access to the full range of economic opportunity negatively affects a woman's ability to provide for her family, create jobs for others, and contribute to global growth.

In addition to the **Framework for Advocacy and Action**, which offers detailed information about how you can effectively advocate for ensuring that all women have access to jobs, capital and skills, **Take Action at Home** has some concrete suggestions about how to engage friends and family on the grassroots level in an effort to convince them of the importance of breaking down barriers that keep women from reaching their economic potential.

Photo: Brent Clark / Alamy Stock Photo

### EQUAL PAY DAY

In March 2021, on Equal Pay Day, two-time World Cup Champion Megan Rapinoe testified via Zoom in front of the U.S. House Oversight Committee in a hearing focused on pay inequalities between men and women. "If that can happen to us, to me," she said, "with the brightest light shining on us—it can, and it does, happen to every person who is marginalized by gender," Rapinoe said. "We don't have to wait. We don't have to continue to be patient. We can change that today. Right now. We just have to want to."

# DIVING DEEP

You've learned how important it is to ensure that women have equal access to economic opportunity at every level: in the workplace and as entrepreneurs. Here is more in-depth information that you can use to up your ante as an advocate on this issue.

## WOMEN ON CORPORATE BOARDS BOOSTS THE BOTTOM LINE

Diverse boards perform better because they are more likely to mirror their customer and client bases, and are less likely to be taken in by "group think." Some companies and sectors get it, but there are still too many that don't. Large companies are more likely to have at least one woman on their board.[77] Of the companies on the Russell 3000 Index, women hold 18% of board seats, an increase from 16% in 2017.[78] At the same time, women hold just 9% of board seats in the 25 companies that went public in 2017, up from 8% in 2016.[79] Twelve of the 25 companies went public with no women, and 80% went public with no women, or only one woman, on their board.[80]

There are both voluntary and mandatory efforts to increase women on boards. The 30% Club focuses on companies voluntarily increasing the number of women on boards and in corporate leadership. Save in exceptional circumstances, The 30% Club does not believe mandatory quotas are the right approach.[82] Led by CEOs and other high-ranking corporate leaders, The 30% Club approach complements individual company efforts and existing networking groups.

In contrast, California law mandates that public companies with headquarters in the state name at least one woman board member/director.[83] The law further mandates that companies with five-member boards have at least two women directors by the end of 2021, and corporations with six or more directors include at least three women.[84] The penalties for failing to comply rise accordingly. Other states are considering similar legislation.

## FINANCING, NETWORKS, & OTHER RESOURCES

Women must have equal access to, and ownership of, productive resources to obtain financing for their businesses. Women are less likely to own land, housing, agricultural equipment, livestock, and vehicles.[85] While 515 million adults gained access to financial and banking services between 2014 and 2017,[86] women were between 7% and 9% less likely than men to have a bank account.[87]

Founders and new ventures need a supportive culture, unbiased policies and laws, availability of financial and human capital, venture-friendly markets for products, and a range of institutional and infrastructural support. In order to create such an ecosystem, government, business, financial institutions, and investors must work together. There are groups bringing together these key actors, such as Y Combinator, which not only provides seed funding to start-ups but makes connections for founders and ensures legal documents are proper,[88] and LaunchTN, a public-private partnership working to facilitate capital formation and nurture Tennessee's entrepreneurial ecosystem.[89]

## PROMOTIONS AND THE GENDER GAP

When we think about corporate gender gaps, there's a tendency to look to the top (how many women in the C-suite?) or at entry level (how many women are being hired?). Those are important junctures in the pipeline. **For every 100 men promoted or hired to a managerial position, only 72 women are promoted or hired.**[90] The gap widens for non-White women.[91] Only 58 Black women are promoted to manager for every 100 men, and only 68 Latinas.[92]

The gender gap in promotions, particularly first promotions, has a long-term effect on women's professional progression. Women are promoted or hired into their first management position 25% less often than men.[93] Fixing this "broken rung" on the corporate ladder would translate to one million more women in management jobs in the U.S. and Canada. Companies can:

- Set targets for the number of women in first-level management jobs
- Require diverse slates of candidates for hires and promotions at the early manager level
- Establish transparent evaluation criteria so employees and managers clearly understand what it takes to earn a promotion

At the same time, it's critical to address **the confidence gap**. *The Confidence Code*[94] documents how women:

- Don't consider themselves as ready for promotions as men do
- Predict they'll do worse on tests
- Underestimate their abilities

Research demonstrates[95] that learning how to act confident is a confidence builder in and of itself. We all need to support other women in their aspirations, and complement women for their smarts and accomplishments, not just their looks.

## MEASURING CORPORATE COMMITMENT

There are key tools for measuring and tracking progress and showcasing a company's commitment to gender equality, such as the **Women's Empowerment Principles (WEPs)** and **EDGE** Certification.

The WEPs[96] were established by the United Nations and the private sector to emphasize the business case – to demonstrate why it is good for the bottom line – for corporate action to promote gender equality and women's empowerment. Over 5,000 companies have signed onto the WEPs, including Alcoa, ANN INC., Bank of America, Coca-Cola entities, Deloitte, Facebook, Hilton, Mastercard, Merck, and Pepsi. The U.S. Chamber of Commerce also promotes the WEPs. Companies that sign the WEPs commit to seven core principles:

1. Establish high-level corporate leadership for gender equality
2. Treat all women and men fairly at work
3. Ensure the health, safety, and well-being of all workers
4. Promote education, training, and professional development for women
5. Implement enterprise development, supply-chain and marketing practices that empower women
6. Promote equality through community initiatives and advocacy
7. Measure and publicly report on progress to achieve gender equality

**Economic Dividends for Gender Equality (EDGE) Certification**[97] is a business certification focusing on metrics and accountability to achieve workplace gender equality. EDGE works with more than 150 companies and organizations in over 40 countries, including the German multinational software corporation SAP, as well as L'Oréal, the Asian Development Bank, and the International Finance Corporation. The EDGE process assesses policies, practices, and data about:

- Equal pay for equivalent work
- Recruitment and promotion
- Leadership development
- Flexible work
- Company culture

There are three stages of EDGE certification, starting from a public commitment to equality and an inclusive workplace culture, to sustained action and measurable gender equality over time.

## FIVE KEY BUSINESS PRINCIPLES

In 2019, the U.S. Business Roundtable redefined the "purpose" of corporations to include serving citizens, not just shareholders, and to becoming a force for change.[98] The Business Roundtable committed to five key principles:

1. Delivering value to customers.
2. Investing in employees by compensating them fairly and providing important benefits, supporting them through training and education to develop new skills for a rapidly changing world, and fostering diversity and inclusion, dignity, and respect.
3. Dealing fairly and ethically with suppliers by serving as good partners to the other companies, large and small, that are part of the supply chain.
4. Supporting the communities in which companies work by embracing sustainable practices.
5. Generating long-term value for shareholders, and committing to transparency and effective engagement with shareholders.[99]

## ROLE MODELS AND TRAILBLAZERS

**C.J. Walker** promoted her products by traveling around the country, eventually establishing Madame C.J. Walker Laboratories to manufacture cosmetics and train beauticians. Madame Walker was one of the first American women to become a self-made millionaire. Walker's life was portrayed in the 2020 TV show *Self Made*. She paved the way for generations of other women entrepreneurs.

**Oprah Winfrey** is not only the host of the highest-rated talk show in TV history, but runs her own TV network, magazine, and production company. She is an Academy Award-nominated actor and philanthropist. The Oprah Winfrey Show ran from 1985 to 2011 and won 16 Daytime Emmy Awards.

**Ela Bhatt** is a pioneer in women's empowerment. In 1972 she founded the Self-Employed Women's Association (SEWA) in India, now with over one million members, as well as India's first women's bank, the Cooperative Bank of SEWA. As many as 93% of all women workers in India work in the informal sector. SEWA is a trade union for poor, self-employed women workers, organizing them in order to

Clockwise from upper left: C.J. Walker; President Barack Obama awards the 2013 Presidential Medal of Freedom to Oprah Winfrey, November 20, 2013; Ela Bhatt; Dolores Huerta is and has always been a fighter for change; Susan Wojcicki, YouTube CEO, at TechCrunch Disrupt SF 2013.

obtain secure work, income security, food security, and social security. SEWA also helps these women understand their bargaining power and offers them new alternatives. Bhatt has been a member of The Elders.

**Susan Wojcicki** is CEO of YouTube. Wojcicki was involved in the founding of Google, and became Google's first marketing manager in 1999. She later led the company's online advertising business and Google's original video service. Wojcicki proposed the acquisition of YouTube by Google in 2006, and has served as CEO of YouTube since 2014. She has an estimated net worth of nearly $500 million.

**Dolores Huerta** is among the most important labor and justice activists in the U.S. An equal partner in co-founding the first farm-workers unions with César Chávez, her contributions have been less recognized. Huerta tirelessly led the fight for racial and labor justice alongside Chavez, becoming one of the most defiant feminists of the 20th century, and she continues the fight to this day.

We met **Lilly Ledbetter** in Chapter One. Nearing retirement, she discovered that she was being paid significantly less than her male counterparts, and had been for many years. She fought a legal battle about the timing of her claims, which she lost when the U.S. Supreme Court ruled for her longtime employer, Goodyear Tire & Rubber. However, her advocacy continued. The U.S. Congress passed the Lilly Ledbetter Fair Pay Act in 2009, which was the first bill signed into law by President Barack Obama.[100]

## SHAREHOLDER ACTIVISM AS A TOOL FOR CHANGE

You may directly or indirectly (if you have a 401K) own stock. But even if you don't, it is important to know about shareholder activism because every shareholder has the right to file proposals that can be voted upon at company annual meetings. This is an effective way for shareholders to influence business operations. Even submitting a proposal can have an impact, as companies sometimes change practices in response to a filing rather than wait for a formal vote to occur.

Here are some examples of successful shareholder activism:

- At the 2019 annual meeting of Alphabet, the parent company of Google, employees, shareholders, and activists focused on issues from workplace rights of contract employees to business practices in China.[101]

- In 2018, Trillium Asset Management filed a groundbreaking proposal urging Nike to address workplace sexual harassment, improve gender diversity, and narrow pay disparity. The proposal was withdrawn when Nike committed to quarterly meetings to discuss results.[103] In 2020, Trillium was instrumental in FedEx's decision to condition its continued sponsorship of the Washington, DC, football team, formerly known as the Washington Redskins, on a name change.[104]

- Arjuna Capital and the New York State Common Retirement Fund filed resolutions at Facebook and Twitter meetings requesting that each company report on enforcing their content policies and police their platforms for harassment.[105] Arjuna has also filed proposals on the gender pay gap in the financial, tech, and consumer retail industries and has prompted numerous policy changes.

# CONCLUSION

Women are critical to economic growth and prosperity, and we must value women's contributions to the economy as equal to men's contributions. We must break down the barriers that exist, whether legal or normative, and create systems and structures that ensure women thrive.

At the same time, the COVID-19 pandemic has magnified what we already knew about care and household work – that it is still predominantly done by women and girls, and that it is undervalued. As we rectify the inequalities of work and pay, we must also confront the issues around care-giving in order to ensure that women and men bear those responsibilities equally.

The next chapter discusses one very real barrier to women's ability to fully participate in economic and public life: the scourge of gender-based violence (GBV). GBV has devastating economic and personal impacts on women, girls, and their families. It also makes it more difficult for women to realize their full potential. As we will see in the next chapter, while GBV takes many forms, there are also many ways to address it and to assist women in overcoming its consequences.

# RESOURCES: Economic/Financial Information Is Power

In every chapter of the book you will find a list of resources that you can refer to when you are formulating your initial questions, doing your research, finding out who has the power to make change, preparing your questions, and making an advocacy plan. Here you will find resources to facilitate your work helping women participate more fully in the economy.

These lists are available/updated at: stepheniefoster.com

## Movies and TV

- **Daring Women Doctors: Physicians in the 19th Century (2020)**. All-women's medical schools were established in the mid-19th century long before women had the right to vote or own property. This film highlights the pioneering and diverse women, as well as the hostility and resistance they faced in pursuing medical education.

- **Dolores (2017)**. Dolores Huerta is among the most important, yet least known, activists in American history. With intimate and unprecedented access to this intensely private mother of 11, the film reveals the raw, personal stakes involved in committing one's life to social change.

- **Good Girls Revolt (2015)**. A miniseries following a group of young women researchers relegated to low-level and low-pay positions in a newsroom in 1969, even though these women were often more talented and better educated than their male counterparts. It follows their fight for writing credit and equal pay. Inspired by the book of the same name, and released on Amazon Video.

- **Hidden Figures (2016)**. The story of three brilliant Black women at NASA who were integral to the U.S. space race. Starring Taraji P. Henson, Octavia Spencer, and Janelle Monáe (she/her/they).

- **Joy (2015)**. A biographical dramedy starring Jennifer Lawrence as Joy Mangano, who started a million-dollar household industry empire.

- **Made by Women podcast,** https://www.senecawomen.com/podcast-made-by-women

- **Made In Dagenham (2010)**. The story of the Ford sewing-machinists strike of 1968 that aimed for equal pay for women in the United Kingdom. Starring Sally Hawkins, Miranda Richardson, Geraldine James, Rosamund Pike, and Andrea Riseborough.

- **Nine-to-Five (1980)**. A movie classic about how secretaries take on their toxic workplaces. Starring Jane Fonda, Lily Tomlin, and Dolly Parton.

- **Norma Rae (1979)**. The film's narrative follows Norma Rae, a factory worker from a small town in North Carolina who becomes involved in unionizing at the textile factory where she works. Stars Sally Field, who received an Oscar for this role.

- **Picture A Scientist (2020)**. Biologist Nancy Hopkins, chemist Raychelle Burks, and geologist Jane Willenbring highlight their own experiences in science, ranging from brutal harassment to years of subtle slights, providing new perspectives on how to make science more diverse and equitable.

- **Self Made: Inspired by the Life of Madame C.J. Walker (2020)**. A Black woman rises from poverty to build a beauty empire and become the first woman self-made millionaire.

- **Triangle Fire (2018)**. It was the deadliest workplace accident in New York City's history. A dropped match on the 8th floor of the Triangle Shirtwaist Factory started a fire that killed 146 garment workers – 123 women and girls and 23 men – who died from the fire, smoke inhalation, or falling or jumping to their deaths.

## Books

- *Brotopia: Breaking Up the Boys' Club of Silicon Valley* **(2018)** by Emily Chang. An exposé on how Silicon Valley became sexist, why it endures, and how women are now speaking up and fighting back.

- *The Confidence Code: The Science and Art of Self Assurance – What Women Should Know* **(2018)** by Katty Kay and Claire Shipman. A book looking at the neuroscience of "the confidence gene" and how we can all become more confident by taking actions and risks.

- *Drop the Ball: Achieving More by Doing Less* **(2018)** by Tiffany Dufu. A memoir on getting more by letting go and not working to get "everything."

- *55, Underemployed and Faking Normal: Your Guide to a Better Life* **(2019)** by Elizabeth White. A practical plan for people in their 50s and 60s who are out of work, having trouble finding a job, and financially unable to retire.

- *Girls Who Run the World: 31 CEOs Who Mean Business* **(2019)** by Diana Kapp. Part biography, part business how-to, this book for teens and young adults showcases success stories of 31 women leading companies like Rent the Runway, PopSugar, and SoulCycle.

- *The Good Girls Revolt: How the Women of Newsweek Sued Their Bosses and Changed the Workplace* **(2013)** by Lynn Povich. The book is based on the lawsuit female employees of *Newsweek* brought against their employer.

- *Hidden Figures: The American Dream and the Untold Story of the Black Women Who Helped Win the Space Race* **(2016)** by Margot Lee Shetterly. The true story of Black women mathematicians at NASA who helped fuel some of America's greatest achievements in space.

- *Lean In: Women, Work, and the Will to Lead* **(2013)** by Sheryl Sandberg. A continuation of Sandberg's 2010 TED Talk, *Lean In* combines personal anecdotes and practical advice on building a satisfying career.

- *Maid in India: Stories of Inequality and Opportunity Inside Our Homes* (2017) by Tripti Lahiri. An honest account of the complex and troubling relations between "the help" and those they serve. [*Author's note: See my book review in the* Huffington Post.[106] ]

## Organizations

- **BRAC**
  BRAC is an international development organization based in Bangladesh, reaching more than 126 million people with its services. While it has programs in education, public health, and disaster relief, BRAC's first program was in microfinance, providing collateral-free loans to mostly women, whose rate of loan repayment is 98%. www.brac.net

- **Career Girls**
  Career Girls is founded on the dream that every girl has access to diverse and accomplished women role models in order to learn from the experiences of those women and to discover her own path to empowerment. Features women role models in fields from architecture to transportation and everything in between. www.careergirls.org

- **Equal Pay International Coalition (EPIC)**
  EPIC acts at the global, regional, and national levels to support governments, employers, and workers' organizations, and other stakeholders in their efforts to take concrete steps to reduce the gender pay gap. Its goal is to close the gender pay gap by 2030. www.equalpayinternationalcoalition.org

- **EQUAL-SALARY Foundation**
  EQUAL-SALARY is a Swiss non-profit organization founded by Véronique Goy Veenhuys, a social entrepreneur and equal-pay advocate who created the concept of an "equal salary" certification, a practical tool that allows companies to verify and communicate that they pay men and women equally for the same role. www.equalsalary.org

- **Grameen Bank (GB)**
  GB provides credit to the poorest in Bangladesh without the need for collateral. This micro-credit banking system is based on mutual trust, accountability, participation, and creativity. As of November 2019, GB has 9.6 million members, 97% of them women. In 2006, GB and its founder, Muhammad Yunus, shared the Nobel Peace Prize for their efforts in creating economic and social development from the ground up. www.grameen.com

- **National Partnership for Women & Families**
  The Partnership's goal is to improve the lives of women through equality, with a focus on advocating for women's health, reproductive rights, and economic justice. It is a national non-profit, non-partisan organization working to change policy and culture through advocacy in both the public and private sectors at the federal, state, and local levels. www.nationalpartnership.org

- **National Women's Law Center (NWLC)**
  NWLC fights for gender justice – in the courts, in public policy, and in our society – working on issues central to the lives of women and girls. NWLC uses the law to change culture, drive solutions, and break down barriers, especially for those who face multiple forms of discrimination, including women of color, LGBTQ people, and low-income women and families. www.nwlc.org

- **Self-Employed Women's Association (SEWA)**
  SEWA is an organization and a movement. As an organization, it is a trade union of poor, self-employed women workers, an unprotected labor force in India. Its goal is to organize women workers for full employment, offering work and economic security. As a movement, its focus is on full employment and self-reliance. www.sewa.org

- **TIME'S UP**
  An independent, non-partisan non-profit, TIME'S UP is focused on changing work culture, companies, and laws in order to create a society free of gender-based discrimination in the workplace and beyond. TIME'S UP wants to eliminate sexual harassment, abuse, and retaliation in the workplace, as well as to remove barriers and increase representation and power for women. The organization's goal is to have better opportunities for success for women in all industries. www.timesupnow.org

- **WEConnect International**
  WEConnect is a global network connecting women-owned businesses to qualified buyers around the world, with a goal to give women the same business opportunities as men. The organization identifies, educates, registers, and certifies businesses that are at least 51% women owned, managed, and controlled by women. www.weconnectinternational.org

- **Wogrammer**
  Wogrammaer (recently acquired by AnitaB.org) shares inspiring stories of women and non-binary individuals working in the tech industry. The diverse people profiled on the site and in articles and podcasts are role models for girls and young women around the world in STEM fields. www.wogrammer.org

- **Women's Business Enterprise National Council (WBENC)**
  WBENC is the largest certifier of women-owned businesses in the United States, and a leading advocate for women business owners and entrepreneurs. www.wbenc.org

## Facts and Figures

- **McKinsey Global Institute**[107]
  McKinsey research includes a 2015 report, *Why Diversity Matters*, which found that companies with more diverse workforces perform better financially. Their 2017 follow-up report, *Delivering through Diversity*, reinforces the link between diversity and company financial performance.

- **The U.S. Women, Peace and Security Index** [108]
  The Georgetown Institute for Women, Peace and Security has compiled this index, the first-ever ranking of women's rights and opportunities across 50 states and the District of Columbia, revealing the vast differences in the status of women across America. The index measures women's inclusion in the economy and politics as well as key aspects of justice and legal protections.

- *The Women's Atlas*[109]
  Currently in its fifth edition (2018), this book by Joni Seager provides a comprehensive and accessible analysis of global data on key issues such as equality, motherhood, women at work, women in the global economy, changing households, domestic violence, lesbian rights, women in government and politics, and more.

- **The World Bank**[110]
  The Gender Data Portal is the World Bank's comprehensive source for the latest sex-disaggregated data covering demography, education, health, access to economic opportunities, public life and decision-making, and agency. The World Bank also issues a bi-annual report *Women, Business and the Law*,[111] which compiles a list of country-specific laws that constrain women and girls.

- **World Economic Forum (WEF) Global Gender Gap Report**[112]
  Since 2006, the WEF Global Gender Gap Report has analyzed the laws and policies of 153 countries and benchmarked their progress against regional and global data that measure gender parity across four dimensions including economic participation. It also compares the relative status of and/or access to economic opportunity for men and women.

These lists are available/updated at: stepheniefoster.com

# NOTES

1    Chaney, Sarah, "Women's Job Losses From Pandemic Aren't Good for Economic Recovery," *The Wall Street Journal*, June 21, 2020, https://on.wsj.com/3fXzzYq.

2    "Nearly 40 Percent of Unemployed Women Have Been Out of Work for 6 Months or Longer," National Women's Law Center, December 2020, https://bit.ly/33X8ujs

3    Hinchliffe, Emma, "14% of Women Considered Quitting Their Jobs Because of the Coronavirus Pandemic," *Fortune*, April 23, 2020, https://bit.ly/36oUSyR.

4    Foster, Stephenie and Markham, Susan, "COVID-19 Demands We Rethink Gender Roles," Diplomatic Courier, https://bit.ly/2Vp3ejW.

5    Woetzel, Jonathan et al, "The Power of Parity," The McKinsey Global Institute, September 1, 2015, https://mck.co/3fW0UtT.

6    Ibid.

7    Savchuk, Katia, "Do Investors Really Care About Gender Diversity?", Stanford Graduate School of Business, September 17, 2019, https://stanford.io/2JDtjco. The study found that if Google had reported that women made up 31% of its workforce, instead of 30%, it could've added $375 million in market value.

8    "Women in Business: Beyond Policy to Progress," Grant Thornton, March 8, 2018, https://bit.ly/2JzCACd.

9    Ebrahimji, Alisha, "Female Fortune 500 CEOs reach an all-time high, but it's still a small percentage," https://cnn.it/39x5eyP.

10   Hunt, Vivian et al, "Diversity Matters," McKinsey & Company, February 2, 2015, https://mck.co/33vks3d; Krivkovich, Alexis et al, "Women in the Workplace 2018," McKinsey & Company, October 23, 2018, https://bit.ly/2JC4ywR.

11   Blumberg, Yoni, "Companies with More Female Executives Make More Money: Here's Why," CNBC, March 2, 2018, https://cnb.cx/3muxfuv.

12   FP Analytics, "Women as Levers of Change," *Foreign Policy Magazine*, https://bit.ly/36skpHp.

13   Menton, Jessica, "Jane Fraser named CEO of Citigroup, becoming the first woman to lead a major Wall Street bank," *USA Today*, September 11, 2020, https://bit.ly/39vc1ZB.

14   The World Bank, "Women, Business, and the Law 2021," 2021, https://wbl.worldbank.org/en/wbl.

15   The World Bank, "Women, Business, and the Law 2018," 2018, https://bit.ly/39DmVwJ.

16   The World Bank, "Women, Business, and the Law 2019," 2019, https://bit.ly/3mueOGi. Also: The World Bank, "Women, Business, and the Law 2021," 2021, https://wbl.worldbank.org/en/wbl.

17   The World Bank, "Women, Business, and the Law 2021," 2021, https://wbl.worldbank.org/en/wbl.

18   The World Bank, "Women, Business, and the Law 2019," 2019, https://bit.ly/3mueOGi.

19   Ibid.

20   The World Bank, "Women, Business, and the Law 2021," 2021, https://wbl.worldbank.org/en/wbl.21 "Single Mother Statistics," Single Mother Guide, https://bit.ly/3mGutm5.

22   "Minimum Wage," National Women's Law Center, https://bit.ly/3ltVUOv.

23   "Turning Promises into Action: Gender equality in the 2030 Agenda for Sustainable Development," UN Women, 2018, https://bit.ly/33vmX5B.

24   Depending on the study you use, women earn about 80 percent of what White men earn; African American women, 66 percent; and, Hispanic women, 60 percent. Over the course of a lifetime, because of the pay gap, the average woman who works outside the home will lose more than $500,000 in earnings, and college educated women will lose $800,000.

25   "Women's Median Earnings as a Percent of Men's, 1985-2016 (Full-time, Year-Round Workers) with Projections for Pay Equity, by Race/Ethnicity," Institute for Women's

Policy Research, November 1, 2017, https://bit.ly/3fV6BbD.

26  Ibid.

27  Schmidt, Samantha, "Study: Wage gap robs Black women of nearly $2 million," *The Washington Post*, July 29, 2020, https://wapo.st/3ltXZdh.

28  "Equal Pay Days," The Equal Pay Today Campaign, http://www.equalpaytoday.org.

29  "The Simple Truth About the Gender Pay Gap Fall 2019 Update," American Association of University Women, 2019, https://bit.ly/39tzyKB.

30  "Turning Promises into Action: Gender equality in the 2030 Agenda for Sustainable Development," UN Women, 2018, https://bit.ly/33vmX5B.

31  Wilson, Chris, "Just How Bad is the Gender Pay Gap? Brutal, When You Look at a Lifetime of Work," *Time* magazine, April 2, 2019, https://bit.ly/3my90eQ.

32  "The Gender Pay Gap Situation in the EU," European Union, https://bit.ly/3qcgy9g.

33  Any Qin, "A Prosperous China Says 'Men Preferred' and Women Lose," *The New York Times*, July 16, 2019, https://nyti.ms/36pTZGe.

34  Ibid.

35  Ibid.

36  Gates, Melinda, "How Rethinking Caregiving Could Play a Crucial Role in Restarting the Economy," *The Washington Post*, May 7, 2020, https://wapo.st/3lsBUM7.

37  Woetzel, Jonathan et al, "The Power of Parity," The McKinsey Global Institute, September 1, 2015, https://mck.co/3fW0UtT.

38  Madgavkar, Anu et al, "COVID-19 and Gender Equality: Countering the regressive effects," The McKinsey Global Institute, July 15, 2020, https://mck.co/2JpkRxu.

39  Ibid.

40  Ibid.

41  See Chapter One; Cindy Robbins, "2019 Salesforce Equal Pay Update," Salesforce, April 2, 2019, https://sforce.co/2VjYfAN.

42  Women's Forum for the Economy & Society, "Daring Circles Women & Business," https://bit.ly/3fXYoDB, citing Kelly, D. et al, "Gem Special Report: Women's Entrepreneurship," Global Entrepreneurship Research Association, 2014 and "World Development Indicators: Women and Development," World Bank, 2018.

43  Women's Forum for the Economy & Society, "Daring Circles Women & Business," https://bit.ly/3fXYoDB, citing Vasquez, E.A. & Frankel, B, "The Business Case for Global Supplier Diversity and Inclusion: The critical contributions of women and other underutilized suppliers to corporate value chains," WEConnect International.

44  Janet's List, https://janetslist.co.uk/.

45  Find this directory at https://www.womenownedlogo.com/buy-women-owned-directory.

46  https://www.minerva.directory/.

47  https://womenalsoknowstuff.com/.

48  https://www.woxnetwork.org/.

49  *Harvard Business Review*, August 26, 2010. 210. [podcast] HBR ideacast. Available at: https://bit.ly/3fVyS1K [Accessed 7 August 2020].

50  "The Key Role of Sponsorship," SLAC, https://stanford.io/39Ay7tM.

51  Greenfield, Rebecca, "The White-Male Mentorship Premium," *Bloomberg News*, August, 2019, https://bloom.bg/2KWY1hc.

52  Ibid.

53  Ibid.

54  Ibid.

55  "The Pledge: I will not be part of all-male panels," https://www.owen.org/pledge/.

56  Green, Jeff, "Men Still Outnumber Women 2-to-1 as Speakers at Conferences," Bloomberg, November 1, 2018, https://bloom.bg/37iKKqw.

57  "Redistribute Unpaid Work," UN Women, https://bit.ly/33ysGrn.

58  "American Time Use Survey Chart," US Bureau of Labor Statistics, last modified

December 20, 2016, https://bit.ly/3qhSSjM.

59 "Women's Domestic Burdens Just Got Heavier with the Coronavirus," *The Guardian*, https://bit.ly/33zQXgL.

60 Featherstone, Liza, "The Pandemic is a Family Emergency," *New Republic*, May 7, 2020, https://bit.ly/39vrfOe; Noguchi, Yuki, "Coronavirus Triple Duty: Working, Parenting, and Teaching From Home," NPR, March 17, 2020, https://n.pr/3oixKIB.

61 Wezerek, Gus and Ghodsee, Kristen, "Women's Unpaid Labor is Worth $10,900,000,000,000," *The New York Times*, March 5, 2020, https://nyti.ms/2HYbsw5.

62 Ibid.

63 "Women's Economic Empowerment in the Changing World of Work," UN Economic and Social Council, December 30, 2016, https://bit.ly/3oghOXo.

64 Vogel, Laura, "Famous Stay-at-Home Dads," Moms.com, https://bit.ly/36pNW4G; see also Donner, Francesca, "The Household Work Men and Women Do, and Why," *The New York Times*, February 2, 2020, https://nyti.ms/2JjxQAW.

65 Johnson, Stefanie and Kirk, Jessica F., "Research: To Reduce Gender Bias, Anonymize Job Applications," *Harvard Business Review*, March 5, 2020, https://bit.ly/3ocpIRf.

66 Omeokwe, Amara, "Study Finds Salary-History Bans Boost Pay for African-Americans, Women," *The Wall Street Journal*, June 18, 2020, https://on.wsj.com/3fY6o7n.

67 "Zurich sees leap in women applying for senior roles after offering all jobs as flexible," November 17, 2020, https://bit.ly/3oexGtq.

68 Goldin, Claudia, and Cecelia Rouse, "Orchestrating Impartiality: The Impact of 'Blind' Auditions on Female Musicians," *The American Economic Review*, 90(4): 715-741, found at Gender Action Portal of Harvard Kennedy School Women and Public Policy Program, https://bit.ly/36rItKq.

69 Amiel, Geraldine, "An In-Person Oral Exam at a Prestigious School was Scrapped – and More Women Were Admitted," *Fortune*, August 26, 2020, https://bit.ly/2JDsiAL.

70 Thomas, Erin, "Your Blind Hiring Process is (Probably) Still Biased. Here's How to Change That," *Fast Company*, June 27, 2019, https://bit.ly/2JuAbIS.

71 Vinetta Project website, https://www.vinettaproject.com/.

72 First Round Capital, http://10years.firstround.com/. This study compares data over a 10-year period.

73 Valentina Zarya, "Female Founders Got 2% of Venture Capital Dollars in 2017," *Fortune*, January 31, 2018, https://bit.ly/2I204PY.

74 Lev-Ram, Michal, "Why 90% of the Investors in This New Silicon Valley Venture Fund Are Women," December 11, 2019, https://bit.ly/2VlPxSE.

75 Mascareenhas, Natasha, "Sarah Kunst's Cleo Capital Raises $3.5 Million To Boost Women Decision Makers In VC," Crunchbase News, August 20, 2019, https://bit.ly/3moxiYC.

76 Next Wave Impact Fund website, https://nextwaveimpact.com/about/.

77 "2020 Women on Boards Gender Diversity Index: 2018 progress of women corporate directors by company size, state and industry sector," 2020 Women on Boards, https://bit.ly/3lshsLe.

78 Ibid.

79 Ibid.

80 Ibid.

81 www.30percentclub.org.

82 Ibid.

83 Groves, Martha, "How California's 'Woman Quota' is Already Changing Corporate Boards," Cal Matters, December 16, 2019, https://bit.ly/33QbXAj.

84 Ibid.

85 Deere, Carmen Diana and Doss, Cheryl R., "The Gender Asset Gap: What do we know and why does it matter?" *Feminist Economics*, 2006 available at Taylor and Francis

Online, https://bit.ly/36q47yK.

86 Demirgüç-Kunt, Asli et al, "The Global Findex Database 2017: Measuring financial inclusion and the Fintech revolution," The World Bank, https://globalfindex.worldbank.org.

87 "2018 Findex Shows No Progress on Global Financial Inclusion Gender Gap," Financial Alliance for Women, May 2, 2018, https://bit.ly/2JqJUjJ.

88 https://www.ycombinator.com/about/.

89 https://launchtn.org/about/. For a list of other accelerators, see "31 Top Accelerators and Incubators for Women," https://bit.ly/3muKUlh.

90 Huang, Jessica et al, "Women in the Workplace 2019," McKinsey and Company, October 15, 2019, https://mck.co/2JtApQT.

91 Ibid.

92 Ibid.

93 Hinchliffe, Emma, "Closing the 'First Promotion' Gender Gap Would Add 1 Million Women to Management," Fortune, October 15, 2019, https://bit.ly/2Vot5s7.

94 The Confidence Code, https://theconfidencecode.com.

95 "Building Confidence," https://www.skillsyouneed.com/ps/confidence.html; Vozza, Stephanie, "Science-Backed Ways to Build Confidence When You Feel Like You're Out of Your League," Fast Company, October 7, 2016, https://bit.ly/37oxvF4.

96 Women's Empowerment Principles, https://www.weps.org.

97 EDGE website, http://edge-cert.org/.

98 "Business Roundtable Redefines the Purpose of a Corporation to Promote 'An Economy That Serves All Americans'," Business Roundtable, August 19, 2019, https://bit.ly/3ohajiy.

99 Ibid.

100 "From the Archives: President Obama Signs the Lilly Ledbetter Fair Pay Act," https://bit.ly/3qhlolR.

101 De Vynck, Gerrit, "Alphabet is Under Pressure from Protestors at its Annual Meeting," Los Angeles Times, June 19, 2019, https://lat.ms/3fUyTTH.

102 Katz, David A. and McIntosh, Laura A., "Corporate Governance Update: Shareholder activism is the next phase of #MeToo," Harvard Law School Forum on Corporate Governance, September 28, 2018, https://bit.ly/39ys60A.

103 Ibid.

104 McCartney, Robert, "Timing of NFL Team's Name Review Tells Real Story," Star Tribune, July 13, 2020, http://strib.mn/33z8E04; Carpenter, Les, "Washington's NFL Team to Retire Redskins Name, Following Sponsor Pressure and Calls for Change," The Washington Post, July 13, 2020, https://wapo.st/37oypkW.

105 "Arjuna Capital and NY State Ask Facebook to Explain Plans for Governing Content," Business Wire, October 30, 2018, https://bwnews.pr/2Vr6ZVL.

106 Foster, Stephenie, "Book Review: Maid in India - All in A Day's Work," Huffington Post, August 14, 2017, https://bit.ly/2JgxET1.

107 www.mckinsey.com.

108 https://giwps.georgetown.edu/usa-index/.

109 Seager, Joni, "The Women's Atlas," Penguin Random House, October 30, 2018, https://bit.ly/37FmD5V.

110 www.worldbank.org.

111 https://wbl.worldbank.org/#.

112 www.weforum.org.

CHAPTER FOUR

# Safety & Security

*Violence is not confined to the battlefield. For many women and girls, the threat looms largest where they should be safest – in their homes.*

António Guterres
Secretary-General of the United Nations

Violence against women and girls is a human rights violation and it is an impediment to women's equality. In every country, women and girls face violence and physical threats, which makes it harder for them to fully participate in society. As the COVID-19 pandemic has shown, crises exacerbate this issue. Although statistics on the prevalence of violence against women and girls are often difficult to capture, the scale is tremendous, the scope is vast, and the consequences for individuals, families, and communities are devastating.

## GENDER BASED VIOLENCE (GBV)

At least 35% of women worldwide have experienced GBV,[1,2] with astronomical prevalence in some countries: 65% of women in Bangladesh, 56% in Equatorial Guinea, and 44% in Sierra Leone report experiencing GBV.[3]

In the U.S., according to the Centers for Disease Control and Prevention (CDC), over 43% of women in the U.S. (approximately 52 million) report experiencing some form of sexual violence over the course of her lifetime.[4]

- One in three women in the U.S. has experienced physical violence by an intimate partner in her lifetime.[5]

- Every minute, 24 people in the U.S. are victims of rape, physical violence, or stalking by a partner, totaling 12 million women and men each year.[6]

- During the pandemic, these cases have increased significantly. San Antonio, Texas, for example, saw a 21% increase in family violence calls, with more than 500 additional calls during the first three weeks of the pandemic, compared to the same period in 2019.[7]

# HOW TO REACH OUT FOR HELP

**If you are in an abusive relationship, or know someone who is, reach out to professionals who can help at the U.S. National Domestic Violence Hotline:**

**1-800-799-SAFE (7233)**

**1-800-787-3224 (TTY)**

**Text: LOVEIS to 22522**

The hotline is staffed 24/7 by trained advocates, and it is confidential and free. It provides immediate support to those calling as well as information about crisis intervention, educational services, and referral services. Help is available in 200 different languages.

The National Domestic Violence Hotline was established in 1996 by the U.S. Violence Against Women Act (VAWA).[8] The Hotline's website, www.thehotline.org, has information about state-level resources as well as specific resources for teens and the LGBTQ+ community.[9]

A multilingual and international directory of domestic violence agencies can be found at www.hotpeachpages.net. This resource has information in 110 languages.

**If you are in immediate danger, call 911.**

## Other Ways to Reach Out for Help

In this era of endless Zoom calls, you can **Signal for Help**, or #SignalForHelp during a video call by using a one-handed gesture to communicate that you feel threatened. The movement involves facing your palm to the camera or person, tucking your thumb into your palm, and folding your four fingers over the top of your thumb. It sends the signal, "Please reach out to me safely."

Credit: Women's Funding Network

1. Palm to camera and tuck thumb

2. Trap thumb

THE VIOLENCE AT HOME SIGNAL FOR HELP

Use this signal to ask for help on a video call without leaving a digital trace.

If you see this sign on a video call, find out how to help below.

#SignalForHelp is a way to ask for help without leaving a digital footprint.

**If you see this gesture**, email, text, or call the person back and ask yes or no questions (would you like me to call 911? Do you need me to call a shelter? Should I look into some services for you? etc.) so they don't have to vocalize their fears while near a potential abuser.

**The Women's Funding Network** has a site with more resources.[10]

The Anti-Violence Project offers a **24-hour English/Spanish** hotline for LGBTQ+ people experiencing abuse or hate-based violence: **Call 212-714-1141.**

- If you go to a pharmacy or drugstore in certain places, you can say the **code word "mask 19"** to the pharmacist, and she or he will call for help.[11]

As you use the internet to search for support and information, be aware of your online safety. It is good practice to use a gender-neutral username on websites, and DO NOT SHARE personal information, including first or last name, home address, or any detailed information. Keep track of any harassment or GBV that occurs online.

## THE MANY FACES AND EFFECTS OF GBV

GBV is not only a violation of an individual's human rights,[12] but it causes physical and mental harm, limits access to jobs and education, and reduces productivity. It is a significant public health challenge with vast social and economic consequences.

The terms **GBV** and **violence against women and girls** are often used interchangeably, but they are different. Both women and men experience GBV, although the majority are women and girls. The term **gender-based** acknowledges that this violence is based on gender norms, control, and unequal power relationships.

GBV takes on many forms, and occurs regardless of ethnicity, race, age, class, religion, and education level. GBV encompasses violence directed against people based on biological sex, gender identity, or perceived adherence to socially defined norms of masculinity and femininity. A report by the CDC found that Black, Hispanic, and Native American women faced a higher rate of physical violence and rape by an intimate partner than White women, as did women in households with a combined income of less than $25,000.[13] This is also true for LGBTQ+ people, as more than 40% of lesbians and 60% of bisexual women have faced intimate-partner rape, violence, or stalking.[14]

GBV is pervasive, and can include:

- Physical, sexual, and psychological coercion and abuse[15]
- Rape[16]
- Domestic violence (also called intimate-partner violence)[17]
- Threats of violence[18]
- Arbitrary deprivation of liberty[19]
- Economic deprivation[20]
- Infanticide[21]
- Child sexual abuse[22]
- Sex trafficking and forced labor[23]
- Elder abuse[24]
- Harmful traditional practices such as early and forced marriage, so-called "honor" killings, and female genital mutilation/cutting[25]

This "real world" behavior is being replicated more and more online, where it can be almost impossible to identify the perpetrators and take legal actions. As an example, according to an Amnesty International study, at least 1 million abusive or problematic tweets were sent to women in 2017, an average of one abusive tweet every 30 seconds.[26] Overall, 10% of all tweets sent to Black women, and 6% sent to White women, were abusive.[27]

## THE COST OF GBV

The cost of GBV is estimated conservatively at 2% of global GDP, which translates to $1.5 trillion,[28] equivalent to the entire Canadian economy.[29] **The U.S. loses $1.8 billion in productivity annually due to GBV**, and 8 million days of paid work.[30] According to the CDC, rape or attempted rape in the U.S. costs a survivor more than $120,000 over the course of her (and sometimes his) lifetime, and represents a total economic burden of almost $3.1 trillion.[31] In a 2010 study, economists calculated that the average cost of a single sexual assault in the U.S. is $240,776, which includes medical bills, legal costs, and lost productivity.[32]

Ensuring that women have equal access to economic opportunity, education, and health care is a fundamental right. GBV holds women and girls back and stunts their ability to excel. We must address GBV to make progress toward those goals and core issues that are critical to a woman's ability to fully participate in society.

- Those who experience GBV experience **limits on their earning potential** because of injury or inability to work as a result of violence.[33]
- They carry an **increased financial burden** for medical and legal services, for relocation expenses, and when seeking refuge from violence.[34]
- Their rates of **physical injury, disability, and death (homicide/suicide)** increase due to GBV, as do negative health outcomes.[35] More than 42% of women who experience intimate-partner violence report an injury as a result of the violence.[36]
- Their **educational achievement is stunted.**[37] If a girl misses school because of GBV, every year of secondary school missed increases the likelihood of child marriage by 6%.[38]

## ADVOCACY AND ACTION: WHAT'S THE FIRST STEP?

In Chapter One, I identified a **Framework for Advocacy and Action.** Let's use that framework in terms of advocacy and organizing to prevent and respond to GBV.

### 1. Identify An Issue You Care About

The general focus for this chapter is the tremendous negative impact of GBV on individuals, families, communities, and businesses, and what can be done to stop GBV and change the culture of violence. You can narrow your focus to, for instance, ensure that there are adequate shelters and emergency services in your community so that those who are suffering from domestic or intimate-partner violence have access to a safe haven. You can also advocate for services that are multilingual.

### 2. Do Current Laws or Programs Prevent GBV and Protect Women and Girls?

This chapter outlines how GBV affects the ability of primarily women and girls to go to school, be productive in their workplaces and jobs, and participate in public life. If you are advocating for more shelters, you should look at whether there are zoning laws that might prohibit shelters in certain parts of your community. You should also look at whether information is available in multiple languages and whether there are effective referral processes in place when police or social workers are called to respond to a domestic-violence report.

### 3. Investigate the Context So You Can Understand the Landscape

This is an especially challenging time. As mentioned above, stay-at-home orders that have accompanied the COVID-19 pandemic have exacerbated domestic violence [39] and are predicted to lead to millions of cases of child marriage, female genital mutilation, and unintended pregnancy.[40] It's important that your advocacy and organizing take that into account and address issues that may come up because of COVID: the inability of survivors to easily report the abuse confidentially, given that they are at home with the perpetrator, and the burdens on government services due to the pandemic.

While every community is different, we know that ensuring that women have access to services for themselves and their families is critical. Those services include:

- Hotlines that are confidential, available 24/7, and multilingual
- Shelters that are secure and provide housing support for families in crisis

We also know that law enforcement must take these crimes seriously. They must:

- Have policies in place to refer women to shelters
- Enforce restraining orders
- Prosecute perpetrators

### 4. Find Out Who Has the Power to Make Change

This will depend on the challenges you encounter. If the issue is zoning, then you will need to work with the local planning department. If it is policy around how police respond, and whether they refer survivors to shelters, then you need to work with the police, social services agencies, and local government officials. In all likelihood, it's a combination of these people and institutions. (See Chapter 1, Step 4.)

### 5. Define Your Interest in This Issue

Once you have identified your issue, and know who has the power to make the necessary changes, it is important to communicate to the person you will be talking to **why this issue is important enough to trigger your actions.** This is a critical step. You will need to decide how to approach this issue and clarify your focus. (See Chapter 1, Step 5.)

If you want to change zoning policies that restrict shelters in a particular neighborhood, then you should identify: 1) the best possible locations (e.g., at the neighborhood level) for shelters, 2) the zoning laws that are at issue, 3) whether there is community support or opposition, 4) the reasons that those zoning restrictions exist, 5) whether there are other, nearby neighborhoods without zoning restrictions, and 6) what specific changes you would make to the regulations.

If you are a woman who has experienced GBV, and needed a shelter or other services, and you are willing to tell your story, that will be very powerful. If not, see if you can find someone who would be willing to talk about their story and the importance of ensuring that shelters are available across your locality. Or see if a local organization that works with shelters can represent the stories of others and discuss the collective impact. Then put together a short summary of what you want to accomplish, your reasoning, and the impact of the change you envision.

### 6. Prepare Your Questions

If you are going to ask the powers that be questions about how to ensure that there are adequate shelters and other services, for example, be prepared to make the case that these services are critical to protect women from GBV and give them an opportunity to build a safer life.

Use the research that indicates those who experience GBV:

- Have limits on their earning potential because of injury or inability to work as a result of violence
- Carry an increased financial burden for medical and legal services, and for relocation expenses when seeking refuge from violence
- Increase their rate of physical injury, disability, death (homicide/suicide), and other negative health outcomes[41]

Know that **American women are killed by intimate partners** (husbands, lovers, ex-husbands, or ex-lovers) **more often than by any other type of perpetrator**, and this type of homicide accounts for approximately 40% to 50% of U.S. femicides.[42] It is important that women be able to safely leave those situations and seek shelter.

Be prepared to discuss the fact that 19% of domestic-violence incidents involve a weapon, and **the presence of a gun** in a domestic-violence situation increases the risk of homicide by 500%.[43]

Review the information in **Diving Deep,** later in this chapter, and the material suggested in the **Resources** section (remember: INFORMATION IS POWER!).

Here are some questions to ask **zoning officials**:

- What are the specific zoning policies?
- Do they prohibit shelters?
- Are there limits on the number of people who can occupy a structure?
- If there are shelters in this neighborhood or others nearby, have there been any complaints filed?
- If so, about what?

Here are some questions to ask **neighborhood organizations**:

- How can the police and local authorities ensure the safety of women and children at the shelters?
- Do people in the neighborhood have specific concerns?
- Are there any security issues that need to be addressed?
- Is there a concern about increased traffic or violence?
- Will a shelter create additional financial costs/increase taxes because police will need to hire or deploy officers to the area in case there are incidents of violence associated with the shelter?

By analyzing the answers to these questions, you will be able to refine your proposed solutions.

## 7. Develop Suggestions for Solving the Challenges You Are Raising

It's important to suggest solutions for the issue you are raising. If you don't, those with power may dismiss you and question your commitment. **The solution you propose doesn't have to be perfect or solve the entire problem.** But putting *something* forward reflects your seriousness and interest in making change. It also gives your effort more focus, which makes it easier for others to organize around it and thus amplify your message. Here are some ideas to get you going:

- If you are concerned about **online violence against women**, organize others to develop a campaign to hold online platforms accountable. This can be a combination of laws to restrict certain content, and a process to review objectionable content "in real time" – as it is posted or shortly thereafter.

- If you are concerned with **early and forced marriage**, advocate for laws that restrict the age of marriage so that both young women and young men cannot marry until they are 18 years old. In the U.S., only a few states prevent child marriages with no exceptions. (See **Resources**, below, for more information on child, early, and forced marriages.)

## 8. Ask Your Questions and Outline Your Suggestions

There are many ways to ask the questions you've developed, and you should use the combination that works for you. You can:

- Send a letter or email.
- Engage on social media about your issue with others who share your views, or with decision-makers.
- Ask in person at meetings or if you see the policy maker in person at an event.
- Make an appointment specifically to talk about the issue, ask your questions, and if appropriate be ready with a concrete ask for the meeting. For example, you can ask the person you are meeting with if they will consider a policy change or sponsor relevant legislation (if needed), or ask if they will commit to looking into the issue and consider your suggestion for action on the issue. **Or at the very least, ask them if you can meet again in a month to discuss progress.**

If you need a script for your conversation, here's a start. You should only address one issue in each phone call, video chat, or letter:

> *Hello, my name is _____, and I am a constituent of President/Governor/Senator _____. I am calling/writing to urge that Senator _____ vote yes (or no) on bill number ___ about processing rape kits in a timely way. Do you know how she will vote?*

Asking questions forces these institutions to gather data in order to answer you. Absent a question, people may not know that their policies and practices don't meet the needs of those facing GBV. Your local government or police department may know the number of arrests it makes each year in domestic violence cases, but not how those cases are resolved or what number of cases aren't prosecuted. **Are large numbers of cases not being prosecuted because victims have been pressured to drop complaints or because rape kits haven't been tested?** An organization may have never looked at whether engaging social workers – in addition to police officers – makes a difference in addressing the root cause of GBV.

Making a suggestion demonstrates your commitment to the issue, and if you've done your homework, the person you are meeting with will at least consider following through on your ideas in some way, or will open up a dialog about how to move forward in another way.

**9. What Next? Follow up!**

Once you have taken all of these steps, keep the pressure on decision-makers so that your issue isn't forgotten. In other words, **following up is important**. This means:

- **MOST IMPORTANT:** Send a thank-you note. In most cases you will want to include a recap of what was discussed.
- Consider working with an "organizing and advocacy partner." This can be a friend or family member who can serve as a sounding board and a collaborator as you strategize and move forward.
- More than likely there will be a number of actions you can take after your initial meeting. Work with your advocacy partner or with the organization you are working with on the issue to come up with a plan of action.
- Ask for another meeting (and while you are at it, get to know the staff who support the decision-maker as they can be helpful in getting that next meeting).
- Monitor the issue and your progress.
- Identify and engage with other individuals who are interested in the issue. Start to organize them to take action.
- Identify and engage with those who can influence the relevant decision-makers on your issue.
- Develop a tracking system if you are trying to get legislation introduced or a policy changed. Include names and pertinent information on:
  - Legislators who are co-sponsors
  - Decision-makers who can change a policy
  - Legislators who (and how many) support you
  - Legislators who (and how many) oppose you (this last item is particularly important!)
- Develop an easy way to report to others interested in your issue about progress, via email, social media, and/or a public website.

## TAKE ACTION IN YOUR DAILY LIFE!

You may decide that the most important thing you can do is **raise awareness at home**. If that is the case, then you can engage people at the grassroots and make the case that people in your community should care about **the safety and security of women and girls**.

**1. Learn about how victims can safely report GBV.**

(See the box at the beginning of the chapter titled HOW TO REACH OUT FOR HELP.) Find out if your local police force has women officers available to speak with victims reporting GBV and if they have social workers on staff to address GBV and its aftermath. Ask if there is training for officers – both men and women – on how to be sensitive when taking a report about GBV and gathering needed information.

Here are two examples of local law enforcement policies to ensure that women feel comfortable reporting GBV.

- In Odisha, India – the 11th largest state in India, with a population of over 46 million – there are kiosks designed to make reporting of domestic violence and sexual assault easier.[44] Instant Complaint Logging Internet Kiosks (iClik) are located next to ATM machines so as to not raise suspicions when women go into police stations.[45] As a result, the reporting of GBV has increased.[46]

## THE DEBBIE SMITH ACT

Debbie Smith became a role model and advocate for expedited testing after **her own rape kit languished for six years**. She recalled an evidence room where "from floor to ceiling, there were nothing but [rape] kits."[48]

As Smith said: "That is what got me started in my advocacy because I knew what the testing of my kit gave me: It gave me freedom. For the first time after the cold hit was found *[a cold hit is when a connection is made between a crime victim and a perpetrator, in the absence of a current investigation (i.e., a cold case)]* because my kit was tested, I took a walk in my own neighborhood. I was able to walk around freely without feeling like maybe he was watching me. The fear was gone."[49]

The State of Virginia eliminated its backlog of **2,665 rape kits** using funds mandated by the Debbie Smith Act.[50] But there is still more work to do. Virginia now requires police to submit rape kits to the state lab within 60 days, but most test results take twice that long, which means three months can go by after a sexual assault before the authorities have any information to act.

Debbie Smith, whose journey through the criminal justice system led to the Debbie Smith Act, which funds testing of backlogged DNA kits, argues for continued funding at a news conference in Washington, DC.

- The New Jersey Division of Criminal Justice has clear policies for police officers when addressing a case of domestic violence,[47] outlining interviewing techniques and how to handle calls from victims.

**2. Donate to, or volunteer at, a GBV program or domestic violence shelter in your community.**

You can donate money to the National Domestic Violence Hotline or local shelters and hotlines. You can donate clothing and toiletries to shelters and other organizations that help women rebuild their lives, find an appropriate outfit for a job interview, and feel normal. You can volunteer your time. Some shelters use volunteers to staff shifts or answer hotline phones.

**3. If you are a man, don't:**
- **Remain silent when women are being disparaged**
- **Participate in "locker room talk"**
- **Laugh at jokes that are sexist**
- **Talk about beating or berating women**

Joking about women, objectifying them, and seeing this as "harmless fun" normalizes misogyny and violence and desensitizes men (especially young men) to these behaviors. This is damaging to both women and men. "Locker room talk" primes men – and women – to think of women as sex objects, and to consider violent behavior as acceptable.[52] Even if men don't consciously think they have less respect for women as a result of engaging in these kinds of conversations, they are internalizing negative and harmful assumptions about women.[53]

**4. Encourage both girls and boys to resolve disputes without resorting to violence.**

Avoid using the phrase "boys will be boys" when boys hit each other to resolve issues or otherwise. The **Scary Mommy** blog and website have good advice about talking to boys about their feelings from a young age and allowing them to see grown men in their lives as vulnerable.[54]

Encourage both boys and girls to:
- Talk about how they are feeling
- Work out conflicts without violence

**5. Use your voice on social media to bring awareness to GBV.**

Use Twitter, Facebook, Instagram, and other platforms to call for an end to GBV. Join others to bring awareness of what GBV looks like around the world, and how members of the social media universe are taking steps to end GBV globally. We have seen the power of #MeToo to highlight sexual assault and harassment across the globe.

- There are annual campaigns to combat GBV and you can tie your advocacy to these campaigns. For example, **16 Days of Activism** Against Gender-Based Violence is an annual international campaign, including events and media, that starts on November 25, the **International Day for the Elimination of Violence Against Women**, and ends on December 10, **Human Rights Day**. The event is an organizing platform around the world for individuals and organizations to call for the prevention and elimination of violence against women and girls.[55] (See more information in **Resources**, below.)

- Be vigilant about **online violence and harassment**. Examples of creative efforts by individual women to address online GBV and harassment include the movie **Netizens**,[56] which exposes the proliferation of cyber-harassment faced by women both on the web and otherwise in their lives. The organization **Glitch** has an online toolkit that outlines practical steps we can all take to address online GBV.[57]

**6. Ask if your employer has a confidential employee-assistance program (EAP) or other ways to support those experiencing GBV.**

If not, ask your employer to establish one. An EAP is a work-based intervention program to assist employees in resolving personal problems that adversely affect job performance. Most EAPs now address a broad range of issues such as child or elder care, relationship challenges, financial or legal problems, wellness matters, and traumatic events, including workplace violence.

## THE IMPORTANCE OF ENGAGING MEN AND BOYS

While it is critically important to empower women and girls with skills and self-confidence, we can't reach gender equality, and address GBV, without engaging men and boys and addressing gender norms. In countries with higher rates of gender equality, men have better health and welfare outcomes, live longer, and enjoy a broader set of career options.[58] Programs that challenge traditional masculinity can produce beneficial health and education outcomes for men – not only reducing violence against women, but often reducing instances of violence between men.[59] It's important that men:

- Understand how gender equality benefits them
- Understand how they can take action that reduces gender inequality
- Address gender norms that underpin inequality

Without engaging men and boys, programs to empower women are not sustainable. There can also be negative repercussions if there isn't a focus on changing men's attitudes towards women. Projects that empower women economically without engaging men can lead to increased violence against women.[60] A 2019 World Bank study found that **when women improve their economic opportunity there can be backlash** from intimate partners and family, and also from community members, when power relationships and social norms around the role of men as providers and women as caretakers are disrupted.[61]

In order to address this shift of power dynamics, successful programs **enlist** the support of community leaders, **ensure** that male family members understand what the training entails, and **facilitate** non-violent conflict resolution and joint decision-making between men and women through discussions on family issues.[62] Other efforts encourage men to take on household roles, or teach them how to address laws that prevent women from working.

These efforts must focus on more than individuals. Programs and policies must work to change norms and societal notions of gender roles. Engaging influential male figures – whether celebrities or political or religious leaders – is important, as is using social media and "edutainment" to bring about broader change.

Mariska Hargitay meets with Vice President (now President) Joe Biden, a proponent of efforts to combat gender-based violence.

#HeForShe is a movement to engage men and boys in gender equality.

# ROLE MODELS AND TRAILBLAZERS

There are many advocates who have either experienced GBV themselves or have had a family member or friend experience GBV.

I've already highlighted one role model – **Tarana Burke** – in Chapter One as an example of effective advocacy. In 2006, Burke began using the phrase "Me Too" to raise awareness of the pervasiveness of sexual abuse and assault in society. This developed into a broader movement in 2017, when women across the globe started using the hashtag **#MeToo** as they followed the reporting about the Harvey Weinstein sexual abuse allegations. Every woman who came forward to tell her story publicly is a role model in this regard.

Another role model is actor and activist **Mariska Hargitay**, best known for her role as New York Police Department Captain Olivia Benson on the NBC drama series "Law & Order: Special Victims Unit." For her role, Hargitay has received multiple awards and nominations, including a Primetime Emmy and a Golden Globe. Hargitay's work on that show led her to establish the Joyful Heart Foundation, an organization that provides support to people who have been sexually abused, which is profiled in the **Resources** section, near the end of the chapter.

There are men who are taking steps to change the culture around GBV. UN Women's **#HeForShe** campaign challenges men and boys "to become change agents towards the achievement of gender equality."[63] Prominent members include: Canadian Prime Minister Justin Trudeau, former Japanese Prime Minister Shinzō Abe, Rwandan President Paul Kagame, Unilever CEO Alan Jope, Vodafone CEO Nick Read, Barclays CEO Jes Staley, University of São Paulo Professor Vahan Agopyan, Kenyatta University Vice Chancellor Paul Wainaina, and Georgetown University President John DeGioia.

## SUMMARY

This chapter outlines **how GBV limits the ability of women and girls to fully participate in society**, discusses the gender norms that underlie these practices, and explains why addressing GBV is critical.

In addition to the **Framework for Advocacy and Action**, which offers detailed information about how you can effectively advocate for laws and policies to prevent and respond to GBV, **Take Action at Home** has some concrete suggestions about how to engage friends and family on the grassroots level in an effort to convince them of the importance of this issue.

# DIVING DEEP

You've learned how important it is to understand and address GBV. Here is more in-depth information that you can use to up your ante as an advocate on this broad issue.

## SEXUAL HARRASSMENT

Sexual harassment,[64] which includes unwelcome sexual advances, requests for sexual favors, and other verbal or physical harassment in the workplace or at school, is widespread and underreported. It can be verbal, physical, or visual. **At least 25%, and perhaps over 80%, of women in the U.S. will experience sexual harassment at work in her lifetime.**[65] Factors that contribute to workplace sexual harassment are:

- Working in a geographically isolated environment[66]
- Working in a male-dominated profession[67]
- Lack of legal immigration status[68]
- Employment in a workplace where there is a significant power imbalance between men and women[69] (from my perspective, that is *almost every* workplace)

Sexual harassers can be supervisors, co-workers, colleagues, friends, acquaintances, prospective employers, students, teachers, and other school officials. While many are frightened or embarrassed to report it, the #MeToo movement has made it possible for more women to speak out about their experiences and be taken seriously.[70]

## In the Workplace

Workplace sexual harassment and assault are not only wrong, they are costly.[71] The employee cost is staggering and personal: victims experience depression and anxiety, loss of confidence, and decreased career opportunities. They are often forced to quit their job, find a new job, navigate unemployment, and/or abandon their career forever. Eighty percent of women who experience sexual harassment leave their jobs within two years (compared to 50% of women who otherwise leave their jobs within two years).[72]

Employers pay a high price, including the loss of talented employees and their skills, legal fees, retraining costs, and damages to the company related to high turnover rates, low morale, and decreased productivity.[73] Companies lose $28,000 (in 2018 dollars) in productivity *per person* for those working on a team affected by harassment.[74]

The need for a sexual harassment policy applies to every type of institution and organization. **A policy addressing sexual harassment is only a first step**, but an important part of developing a workplace culture that values every employee's contribution. Organizations must have clear standards for behavior, consistent and effective training programs, and policies and processes for addressing complaints. They also must support those who experience harassment. Everyone needs to understand the processes for filing complaints and know, at least in general, what steps will be taken once a complaint is filed. These processes must be transparent and they must protect privacy for the complainant and the alleged perpetrator.

### Questions to Ask Your Employer

These questions about process and policies addressing sexual harassment are appropriate for any organization you are affiliated with:

- How does the organization address claims of sexual harassment?
- What is the sexual harassment policy?
- How do people report sexual harassment?
- Is there a mechanism to go "higher up" if the sexual harasser is their boss, or in management?
- How do you ensure that complainants are safeguarded?
- Do you keep statistics about the number of complaints filed and how they are resolved?
- How can other resources be made available to complainants, such as counseling, an employee-assistance program, or other services?

## SEXUAL HARASSMENT IN THE SERVICE INDUSTRIES

Sexual harassment is an issue everywhere, but women working in service industries often aren't as able to safely speak out when it happens to them.[75] Over 75% of women working at McDonald's reported experiencing at least one form of unwanted or offensive sexual harassing behavior on the job, 66% report experiencing at least two types of harassing behaviors, and 25% experiencing *eight or more* forms of harassment.[76] While nearly 70% of these workers took proper steps to report this behavior, they faced significant backlash. Over 70% faced some form of punishment after reporting and, 42% lost income as a result of being fired, denied a raise or a promotion, or having hours cut.[77]

More than 5,000 hotels and resorts have given hotel workers security devices to help prevent sexual harassment on the job.[78] Some of the devices are panic buttons that signal for help, some make loud noises to alert passers-by that something is wrong. Hotel unions have been pushing strongly for these kinds of safety measures since the birth of the #MeToo movement in late 2017.[79]

## At School

There is a lack of comprehensive data on school-based sexual violence,[80] but we know that approximately 15 million adolescent girls experience forced sex.[81] In the U.S., 29% of those who report sexual assault were traveling to and from work or school, and 7% were at school when they were assaulted.[82] Girls are often coerced by male teachers to exchange sex for grades, or for "payment" of school-related expenses.[83] In Haiti, among girls ages 13 to 17 reporting sexual abuse, school was the second most common place the abuse occurred, and more than a quarter of underage women who were paid for sex reported that most often it happened at a school.[84]

Further, girls are much more likely than boys to be bullied at school, and are twice as likely to be cyberbullied.[85] In the U.K., 20% of girls reported they had been "socially excluded," while only 10% of boys reported being treated the same way.[86] Studies show that students who were bullied received lower test results than those who hadn't been bullied.[87]

Social media and the ubiquity of cell phones has increased sexual harassment and sharing of sexual images. Sexting – the texting of sexual images – is increasingly common among teenagers. More than 25% of teens have received a sext, nearly

15% have sent one, and 12% have forwarded a sext without consent.[88]

**Questions to Ask School Administrators**

As a parent, student, or teacher, you should ask how violence in school is addressed so that school is a place of learning, not fear. For example, ask:

- How do you ensure that your school is free from violence, harassment, and bullying?
- What is the process for reporting GBV incidents?
- How do you address reports of GBV at school?
- Do you monitor campus to ensure students feel safe everywhere?
- Do you keep sex-disaggregated data on GBV at school?
- Is there a process for safeguarding for complainants?

## VIOLENCE AGAINST WOMEN IN POLITICS

Violent threats and actions are used to deter a woman's right to participate in politics, and are among the most serious challenges to women's political rights today.[89] The goal of this type of violence is to make any woman think twice about participating in politics.[90]

- **During the electoral cycle** violence is directed against women who are running for office, working at polling places, attending campaign rallies, talking to voters, or voting.
- **When women are in office**, violence is used to silence or intimidate them or drive them out of politics. In 2019, **Karina García**, a mayoral candidate in Suarez, Colombia, was murdered while campaigning for office,[91] and British **MP Jo Cox** was murdered on her way to an official event.[92]
- **Within political parties**, women can be pressured to have sex in order to be considered for leadership positions (called "sextortion"). This creates reputational risks for all women in political parties as many people believe that any woman in a leadership role "traded favors" to get there.

Violence against women in politics takes many forms. According to the Inter-Parliamentary Union, virtually every woman member of parliament has experienced psychological violence as they carry out their work. One-third have suffered economic violence, 25% physical violence, and 20% sexual violence. These attacks are also directed at appointed officials and other public figures. Here are some recent examples.

- On the steps of the U.S. Capitol, in 2020, **Representative Alexandria Ocasio-Cortez** was called a "fucking bitch" by one of her colleagues, Representative Ted Yoho.[95]
- During the COVID-19 pandemic, a 32-year-old man was arrested for making death threats on social media against two high-profile women elected officials: **Michigan Governor Gretchen Whitmer** and **Michigan Attorney General Dana Nessel**.[96] Women public-health officials have recently been attacked on social media for doing their jobs: dispensing advice on how to lessen the spread of the coronavirus.[97] Several have since left their posts.[98]
- Violence against women journalists, such as **Ghada Oueiss**, has included fake/doctored nude pictures posted on Twitter. **Ola Al-Fares**, a Jordanian lawyer

and journalist, has been repeatedly taunted with claims that her success was due to her providing sexual favors.[99]

These threats are effective. 80% of Australian women are **less likely to consider entering politics** after seeing how the media treated and portrayed **Julia Gillard**, the country's first woman Prime Minister.[100]

These attacks increasingly occur online, where harassment and violence are often anonymous and can develop a mob dynamic. Violence on social media platforms includes direct or indirect harassment, threats of physical or sexual violence, privacy violations such as doxing (uploading private, identifying information publicly), and sharing of sexual or intimate images without consent. Fewer than half of the cases of online violence reported to authorities have been investigated.[101] **Women under 30 are most likely to experience online violence.**[102] Online violence can and does escalate. As an example, the man who murdered British MP Jo Cox had stalked her online for months.[103]

### Questions to Ask Political Party Leaders

If you are active in politics, or concerned about the impact that violence has on women's political participation, you should ask questions of party leaders:

- Do you have a code of conduct regarding the use of language on social and traditional media?
- Do you have a policy against sextortion?
- What is the process for making complaints about violence against women by other party leaders, or party activists?
- What support do you provide for women officials, either elected or appointed, who are being harassed or stalked (whether online or in person)?
- How do you work with other political party leaders to address these issues?

As part of its Not the Cost campaign,[104] the National Democratic Institute developed **think10, a safety-planning tool** that consists of a self-assessment questionnaire that women can use to review their personal and professional vulnerabilities. The answers are used to calculate each individual's overall risk while being a politically active woman in 172 different countries, allowing them to then take informed steps to enhance their safety.[105]

A few countries have laws criminalizing political violence and harassment. Bolivia was the first country to respond to an increase in violent acts against women in politics, with legal reforms passed in 2012.[106] The Inter-American Commission of Women published a model law in 2017 aimed at combating violence against women in political life.[107] Given the prevalence of this type of violence, laws to address the issue need to be enacted, and this is a topic in need of advocacy and action.

## CHILD, EARLY AND FORCED MARRIAGE

Child, early, and forced marriage (CEFM) is defined as a formal marriage, or informal union, where one or both parties are under 18. Globally, at least 12 million girls under 18 marry each year.[108] In sub-Saharan Africa, 40% of young women marry before the age of 18.[109] In South Asia it's 30%.[110]

CEFM increases the likelihood by 50% that girls will drop out of school. It doubles (compared to married adults) a girl's chances of living in poverty and triples the likelihood she will be beaten by her spouse. Further, when these girls become pregnant, they are at higher risk of dying in childbirth, which is the primary cause of death for young women aged 15-19.[111]

While there are laws against CEFM in 153 countries, the majority of those countries allow exceptions, and local social norms often override legal prohibitions.[112]

- In the U.S., there is no federal law prohibiting child marriage[113] and 13 states have no minimum marriage age.[114] Between 2000 and 2015, **200,000 young women under 18 were married**.[115] As of 2021, only seven states,[116] the U.S. Virgin Islands, and American Samoa[117] have banned child marriage. In 2018, Delaware became the first state to ban marriage for anyone under 18, even with parental consent. New Jersey was next, in 2019.[118]

Advocates are working to address the issue in other countries. In July 2019, the Mozambican Parliament voted unanimously to criminalize child marriage.[119] Under the new law, adults who marry a child can be imprisoned for eight to 12 years, and a person who facilitates child marriage can face two to eight years in prison.[120] This follows a landmark ruling in South Sudan that annulled the marriage of a 16-year-old girl.[121]

## FEMALE GENITAL MUTILATION OR CUTTING (FGM/C)

FGM/C is any partial or total removal of the external female genitalia or any other injury of the female genital organs for nonmedical reasons.[122] Girls and young women are most at risk of being subjected to these procedures between birth and age 15.[123] FGM/C is most prevalent in northern and central Africa, in the southern Sahara, and in parts of the Middle East and Asia.[124] FGM/C is illegal in the U.S. and many other countries, but as many as 140 million girls and women alive today have been cut.[125] More than 513,000 girls and women in the U.S. have experienced or are at risk of FGM/C.[126] Some immigrants to the U.S. (and Western Europe) practice FGM/C, or send their daughters to their homeland for FGM/C.

There are complex reasons for FGM/C, with social acceptance the most common reason. Others believe that FGM/C increases men's sexual pleasure, ensures a woman remains a virgin until marriage, or serves as a rite of passage to womanhood.[127]

FGM/C has no health benefits but has measurable, negative, long-term physical, mental, and sexual health impacts.[128] Long-term problems include infection, an increased risk of HIV and sexually transmitted disease, urinary problems, painful and prolonged menstrual periods, problems involving intercourse, depression and anxiety, fistula, prolonged labor, and higher risk for C-sections.[129] Women who have children after FGM/C often give birth to infants with low birth weight and breathing problems.[130]

Some countries have been successful in ending the practice of FGM/C. Currently, at least 14 of 27 members of the European Union have banned FGM/C, and as of 2018, Guinea Bissau, Kenya, and Uganda had criminalized the transport of young women across borders for FGM/C. In other places, rates have dropped. For example, in Egypt until recently, 96% of women 45 to 49 years old were cut, but after 2014 the percentage dropped to 81% among women 15 to 19 years old.[131] Successful efforts to end or reduce FGM/C have the following in common.[132]

- Individuals from the community are the trainers and educators. Many programs use respected local women to teach other girls and women in their communities about the harmful effects of FGM/C.

- Efforts focus on community needs and strengths.
- The programs and the leaders of organizations respect the traditions and social structure of the community, and develop alternatives to FGM/C. Program participants earn community trust so that sensitive issues like FGM/C can be discussed honestly.

## TRAFFICKING AND FORCED LABOR

The International Labour Organization estimates that close to $150 billion in annual profits are tied to forced labor, and **approximately 21 million people worldwide are victims of trafficking (or modern-day slavery)**.[133] Trafficking has devastating consequences. Trafficking includes both sex trafficking and compelled labor.[134] Women and men can be victims of trafficking regardless of whether they were transported to the exploitative situation, previously consented to work for a trafficker, or participated in a crime as a direct result of being trafficked.

When an adult engages in a commercial sex act as the result of force, fraud, or coercion that person is a victim of **sex trafficking**.[135] Those involved in recruiting, harboring, transporting, or maintaining a person for that purpose are guilty of sex trafficking. Both women and men can be victims of sex trafficking, but most are women and girls. **Child sex trafficking** occurs when a child (under 18 years of age) is recruited to perform a commercial sex act.[136] Force, fraud, or coercion is not necessary for the offense to be considered human trafficking.

**Forced labor or labor trafficking** occurs when a person uses force or physical threats, psychological coercion, abuse of the legal process, deception, or other coercive means to compel someone to work.[137] Migrants are particularly vulnerable to this form of human trafficking, but individuals also may be forced into labor in their own countries.[138] Women victims of forced or bonded labor, especially women and girls in domestic servitude, are often sexually abused or exploited as well.[139] Forced child labor occurs when children live in slavery or slavery-like situations against their will.[140]

**Bonded labor** is a form of coercion used by traffickers in both sex trafficking and forced labor.[141] Some workers who inherit debt automatically become bonded laborers. For example, in South Asia it is estimated that there are millions of trafficking victims working to pay off their ancestors' debts.[142] Workers are often charged recruitment fees and exorbitant interest rates, making it difficult, if not impossible, to pay off the debt.[143]

**Involuntary domestic servitude** describes a situation in which a person is recruited to work in a private residence but is not free to leave, is abused, and is underpaid, if paid at all.[144] Many domestic workers do not receive basic benefits and protections, including days off.[145] Moreover, their ability to move freely is often limited, and employment in private homes increases their isolation and vulnerability.[146] Domestic workers, mostly women, confront various forms of abuse, harassment, and exploitation. When the employer of a domestic worker has diplomatic status and enjoys immunity from civil and/or criminal jurisdiction, the likelihood of domestic servitude is higher.[147]

**The recruitment of child soldiers as combatants, or for other forms of labor**, by armed forces – through force, fraud, or coercion – is against the law and is considered human trafficking.[148] Perpetrators may be government forces, paramilitary organizations, or rebel groups.[149] Many children in conflict-affected areas are forcibly abducted to be used as combatants, or as porters, cooks, messengers, or spies.[150] Girls and young women can be forced to "marry" or be raped by commanders and male combatants. Child soldiers are often sexually abused or exploited by armed groups.[151]

## WHAT IS YOUR SLAVERY FOOTPRINT?

You may want to research the laws mandating that companies carefully track what happens in their supply chains.[152] In addition to legal fines, a company's role – however indirect – in human trafficking can and does impact its brand and bottom line. According to a 2015 survey, 66% of global consumers were willing to pay more for sustainable and socially responsible goods.[153]

End Slavery Now[154] produces a slave-free buying guide and offers other suggestions for purchasing slave-free goods. They link to the **Slavery Footprint** survey, which asks the question, "How Many Slaves Work For You?" By answering 11 questions about your consumer spending habits, they will calculate your consumption of common household items created by forced labor and child labor, and produce a graphical "footprint" of how many slaves are required to maintain your personal lifestyle.

## CONCLUSION

Gender-based violence (GBV) is a real barrier to women's ability to fully participate in economic and public life. It has devastating economic and personal impacts on women, girls, and their families. It also makes it more difficult for women to realize their full potential. While GBV takes many forms, there are also many ways to address it and to assist women in overcoming its consequences.

The COVID-19 pandemic, and the stay-at-home orders that have accompanied it, has magnified GBV and created a "shadow pandemic." During the pandemic, these cases have increased significantly across the globe.

The next chapter will address the importance of women's political participation – as candidates, office holders, and voters – to address policy issues, such as GBV, as well as increased access to economic opportunity, education, and health care.

# RESOURCES: GENDER BASED VIOLENCE
## Information Is Power

In every chapter of the book you will find a list of resources that you can refer to when you are formulating your initial questions, doing your research, finding out who has the power to make change, preparing your questions and making an advocacy plan plan. Here are resources related to GBV.

These lists are available/updated at: stepheniefoster.com

## Movies and TV

- **Anita: Speaking Truth to Power (2013).** A profile of Anita Hill, the lawyer who challenged Clarence Thomas' nomination to the U.S. Supreme Court and ignited a political firestorm about sexual misconduct and power in the workplace. Written and directed by Freida Lee Mock.

- **Bombshell (2019).** A feature film based on the accounts of the women working at Fox News who helped expose decades of sexual harassment by the company's CEO, Roger Ailes. Starring Charlize Theron, Nicole Kidman, and Margot Robbie.

- **Difret (2014).** Based on the true story of a 14-year-old Ethiopian girl who resisted abduction in her rural village by men perpetrating the ritualized tradition of bride napping, or kidnapping a woman for marriage. While defending herself she accidentally kills her intended husband, for which she is sentenced to death.

- **El Traspatio (2009).** A fictional account of the true-life story of an unending series of murders of young women in Ciudad Juarez, Mexico, which began in 1996.[155] Most of the victims are low-paid laborers who have been drawn to the town by the possibility of work at American-owned factories.

- **The Greatest Silence (2007).** Stories of women who suffered rape and mutilation during the brutal war in Congo.

- **Mrs. Goundo's Daughter (2008).** This film documents Mrs. Goundo's fight to remain in the U.S. and avoid deportation to Mali in order to prevent her daughter from undergoing female genital mutilation.

- **GTFO (2015).** A documentary directed and produced by Shannon Sun-Higginson about sexism and women in the world of video gaming.

- **I Am Evidence (2017).** Through the stories of four survivors as they navigate the criminal justice system, the movie exposes the number of untested rape kits throughout the U.S. and reveals how the system has mistreated sexual-assault survivors. Produced by Mariska Hargitay.

- **Netizens (2018).** After their lives are disrupted by online harassment and privacy violations, this movie follows three women as they seek justice.

- **NEVERTHELESS (2019).** This film follows the stories of seven individuals who have experienced sexual harassment in the workplace or at school. Focusing on a writer's assistant on a top TV show, a technology company

CEO, a 911 dispatcher, and others, the film shines a light on the ways in which we can shift our culture and rebuild.

- **North Country (2005).** Charlize Theron and Frances McDormand were both nominated for Academy Awards for their work in this film about women working at an iron mill who are constant targets of sexual harassment and humiliation by their male co-workers. Based on the book *Class Action: The Story of Lois Jenson and the Landmark Case That Changed Sexual Harassment Law.*

- **Room (2015).** Brie Larson won an Academy Award for her portrayal of a woman locked in an 11-foot-square room with her young son, born in captivity and fathered by the man who abducted her. Loosely based on an Emma Donoghue novel, which was itself based on a real-life story about a man who for 24 years confined his daughter in his basement, where she gave birth to seven children fathered by him.

- **The Stoning of Soraya M. (2009).** Disturbing movie about a woman being stoned to death. Stars Academy Award nominee Shohreh Aghdashloo, and Mozhan Marnò.

- **The Vagina Monologues (2002).** Based on writer/performer V's (formerly Eve Ensler's) play of the same name, this film portrays women talking candidly about their views and feelings toward their own bodies and about sex.

- **Water (2005).** Set in colonial India against Gandhi's rise to power, this is the story of eight-year-old Chuyia, who is widowed and sent to a home to live in penitence. Directed by Deepa Mehta.

## Books

- *Crash Override: How Gamergate (Nearly) Destroyed My Life, and How We Can Win the Fight Against Online Hate* (**2017**) by Zoë Quinn (they/them). Through their story as the target of what would later be known as "Gamergate," former video game developer Quinn provides an up-close look at how the internet affects our lives and culture, and offers practical tips for keeping yourself safe online.

- *Know My Name* (**2019**) by Chanel Miller. Miller recounts being sexually assaulted in January 2015 on the grounds of Stanford University, its impact on her and her family, and the subsequent court case against Brock Turner.

- *Rage Becomes Her: The Power of Women's Anger* (**2019**) by Soraya Chemaly. Chemaly argues that the rage women feel – from the misogyny and sexism they encounter daily – is not only justified, it is part of the solution.

- *She Will Rise: Becoming a Warrior in the Battle for True Equality* (**2020**) by former U.S. Representative Katie Hill. Hill addresses the events that led her to give up her congressional seat, and the personal and professional aftermath. Covers difficult topics: abuse, depression, family secrets, and trauma.

- *She Said* (**2019**) by Jodi Kantor and Megan Twohey. Recounts how two *New York Times* reporters broke the story of Harvey Weinstein.

# Organizations

- **U.S. National Domestic Violence Hotline:**
  1-800-799-SAFE (7233)
  1-800-787-3224 (TTY)
  The hotline is staffed 24/7 by trained advocates, and is confidential free of cost.

- **A multilingual and international directory** of domestic violence, this resource has information in 110 different languages. www.hotpeachpages.net

- **A Call to Men**
  A Call to Men is a violence-prevention organization that focuses on issues of manhood, male socialization and its intersection with violence, and preventing violence against all women and girls. www.acalltomen.org

- **The Global 16 Days Campaign**
  Coordinated by the Center for Women's Global Leadership, 16 Days is an organizing platform around the world for individuals and organizations to call for the prevention and elimination of violence against women and girls. www.16dayscampaign.org

- **Dress for Success**
  Dress for Success is a global non-profit that empowers women to achieve economic independence by providing a network of support, professional attire, and tools to help women succeed. Dress for Success has a presence in almost 150 cities in 25 countries and has helped over 1.2 million women work towards self-sufficiency. www.dressforsuccess.org

- **FUTURES Without Violence**
  FUTURES provides groundbreaking programs, policies, and campaigns to empower individuals and organizations working to end violence against women and children. FUTURES trains professionals (doctors, nurses, judges, and athletic coaches) on improved responses to violence and abuse. It also works with advocates and policymakers to build sustainable community leadership and educate people about the importance of respect and healthy relationships. www.futureswithoutviolence.org

- **Glitch**
  Glitch works to end online abuse by focusing on increasing responsible digital citizenship across all online users and instilling these beliefs: that the online community is as real as the offline one and that we all should be working together to make it a better place. www.fixtheglitch.org

- **HarassMap**
  HarassMap is a mobile and online technology non-profit that uses interactive mapping to try to reduce the social acceptability of sexual harassment throughout Egypt. Activists and organizations in numerous countries are currently working to set up their version of HarassMap.
  https://harassmap.org/en/

- **HeForShe**
  A global solidarity movement for the advancement of gender equality,

HeForShe seeks to involve men and boys in achieving equality by encouraging them to document their stories about taking action against negative gender stereotypes and behaviors. www.heforshe.org #heforshe

- **Hollaback**
  Hollaback is a bystander intervention, conflict de-escalation, and harassment-prevention campaign that began in New York City to photograph and document street and subway harassment and post those images on the internet. Hollaback provides training on each of these subjects. www.ihollaback.org

- **Joyful Heart Foundation**
  Founded by Mariska Hargitay, Joyful Heart is a national organization with a mission to transform society's response to sexual assault, domestic violence, and child abuse, support survivors' healing, and end violence through education and advocacy efforts. www.joyfulheartfoundation.org

- **Matthew Shepard Foundation**
  Matthew Shepard was the victim of one of the United States' most notorious anti-gay hate crimes. Started by Matthew's parents, the Foundation has a mission to amplify Matthew's story in order to inspire communities to embrace the dignity of all people. Their work helped pioneer the first U.S. federal hate-crime law in 2009. www.matthewshepard.org

- **1 in 6**
  1 in 6's mission is to provide information to and support for men who have had unwanted or abusive sexual experiences, as well as to help the friends, families, and partners of these men. www.1in6.org

- **Promundo**
  Working to advance gender equality and create a world free from violence, Promundo promotes activities that engage men and boys in partnership with women, girls, and individuals of all gender identities. www.promundoglobal.org

- **RAINN (Rape, Abuse and Incest National Network)**
  RAINN is the United States' largest anti-sexual violence organization. Volunteers who staff RAINN's national sexual-assault hotline, 800-656-HOPE, work in partnership with more than 1,000 local sexual-assault service providers across the country. RAINN also operates the Safe Helpline for the Department of Defense. www.rainn.org

- **SafeBAE (Before Anyone Else)**
  SafeBAE is a survivor-founded, student-led organization whose mission is to end sexual assault among middle- and high-school students. As the only national peer-to-peer organization of its kind, it offers teens the tools to become activists and shift school culture by raising awareness about dating violence, sexual harassment and assault, affirmative consent, safe bystander intervention, survivor care, and rights under Title IX. https://safebae.org/

- **Take Back the Night Foundation**
  Take Back the Night is one of the earliest worldwide efforts to combat sexual

violence and violence against women. A 100% volunteer organization, the foundation seeks to end all forms of sexual violence by fostering the creation of safe communities and respectful relationships through awareness, events, and initiatives. www.takebackthenight.org

- **V-Day**
  A global movement to end violence against all women and girls, V-Day works at the intersection of art and activism to shatter taboos, create space for women and the most marginalized, and initiate community-led culture and system change. www.vday.org

## Facts and Figures

- **The U.S. Women, Peace and Security Index**[156]
  The Georgetown Institute for Women, Peace and Security has compiled this index, the first-ever ranking of women's rights and opportunities across 50 states and the District of Columbia, revealing the vast differences in the status of women across America. The index measures women's inclusion in the economy and politics, as well as key aspects of justice and legal protections.

- *The Women's Atlas*[157]
  Currently in its fifth edition (2018), this book by Joni Seager provides a comprehensive and accessible analysis of global data on key issues such as: equality, motherhood, women at work, women in the global economy, changing households, domestic violence, lesbian rights, women in government and politics, and more.

- **WomanStats Project**[158]
  WomanStats investigates the link between the security and behavior of states and the situation and security of women within those states. The project is developing a comprehensive database on these topics. Their database is the largest cross-national compilation of data, statistics, and maps on the status of women worldwide, with information on over 350 variables for 176 different countries.

These lists are available/updated at: stepheniefoster.com

# NOTES

1   World Health Organization, et al., "Violence Against Women Prevalence Estimates, 2018," March 2021, https://who.canto.global/s/KDE1H?viewIndex=0

2   "Facts and Figures: Ending violence against women," UN Women, lasted updated November, 2019, https://bit.ly/37or1pA

3   Joni Seager, *The Women's Atlas*, Penguin Books, updated edition, October 30, 2018.

4   Smith, Sharon G. et al., "The National Intimate Partner and Sexual Violence Survey: 2015 Data Brief – Updated Release," Atlanta: Centers for Disease Control and Prevention, November, 2018, https://bit.ly/33FgrcS

5   Ibid.

6   "Sexual Violence, Stalking, and Intimate Partner Violence Widespread in the US," Center for Disease Control, December 14, 2011, https://bit.ly/36uA7Sj

7   Medina, Mariah, "San Antonio Police See 21% Increase in Family Violence Call Volume Compared to This Time Last Year," KENS5, updated March 26, 2020, https://bit.ly/3oi 3UUt

8   National Domestic Violence Hotline, www.thehotline.org

9   Ibid., https://www.thehotline.org/resources/victims-and-survivors/#orgs

10  Bobb, Brooke, "'Signal for Help' Is a New Tool for Abuse Victims During the Coronavirus Lockdown and Beyond," *Vogue*, April 28, 2020, https://bit.ly/36xNyB7; Women's Funding Network, www.womensfundingnetwork.org/signalforhelp

11  Kottasova, Ivana, "Women are Using Code Words at Pharmacies to Escape Domestic Violence During Lockdown," CNN, April 6, 2020, https://cnn.it/3mwIse5

12  Under the key international treaty addressing GBV, the Istanbul Convention, GBV is defined as a human rights violation and a form of discrimination against women. "Council of Europe Convention on Preventing and Combating Violence Against Women and Domestic Violence," Council of Europe Treaty Office, 2011, https://bit. ly/3g1vTEZ

13  Breiding, M.J. et al., "Intimate Partner Violence in the United States – 2010," National Center for Injury Prevention and Control, Centers for Disease Control and Prevention, 2014, https://bit.ly/3qjnlxX

14  Ibid.

15  "Violence Against Women Fact Sheet," World Health Organization, 2014, https://bit. ly/3ohIerK

16  Ibid.

17  Ibid.

18  Ibid.

19  Ibid.

20  Ibid.

21  "United States Strategy to Prevent and Respond to Gender-based Violence Globally," USAID, Department of State, 2012, https://bit.ly/2JBcsXt

22  Ibid.

23  Ibid.

24  Ibid.

25  Ibid.

26  Amnesty International, "Women Abused on Twitter Every 30 Seconds - New Study," Amnesty International, December, 2017, https://bit.ly/39zwqwF

27  Ibid.

28  "The Economic Costs of Violence Against Women," UN Women, September 21, 2016, https://bit.ly/3qnrOzB

29  Ibid.

30  Maurer, Roy, "When Domestic Violence Comes to Work: 65 percent of employers don't have a plan for domestic violence," Society of Human Resource Management, https://

bit.ly/3g7iUBJ

31   Merrifield, Clark, "The Multi-Trillion Dollar Cost of Sexual Violence: Research roundup," Journalist's Resource, April 19, 2019, https://bit.ly/2Vrac7I

32   "McCollister, Kathryn E. et al., "The Cost of Crime to Society: New crime-specific estimates for policy and program evaluation," US National Library of Medicine National Institutes of Health, published online January 13, 2010, https://bit.ly/33CoqHq

33   "Violence Against Women," World Health Organization, November 29, 2017, https://bit.ly/33BLyWC

34   "United States Strategy to Prevent and Respond to Gender-based Violence Globally," USAID, Department of State, 2012, https://bit.ly/2JBcsXt

35   "World Report on Violence and Health: Summary," World Health Organization, 2002, https://bit.ly/37rFlOe

36   "Violence Against Women," World Health Organization, November 29, 2017, https://bit.ly/33BLyWC

37   Wodon, Q. et al., "Economic Impacts of Child Marriage: Global Synthesis Report," The World Bank and International Center for Research on Women, 2017, https://bit.ly/3oecoMk

38   Ibid.

39   Foster, Stephenie and Markham, Susan, "Covid-19 Demands We Rethink Gender Roles," *Diplomatic Courier*, May 21, 2020, https://bit.ly/2Vp3ejW

40   "Millions More Cases of Violence, Child Marriage, Female Genital Mutilation, Unintended Pregnancy Expected Due to the COVID-19 Pandemic," The United Nations Population Fund, April 28, 2020, https://bit.ly/36xQqxT

41   "Violence Against Women Fact Sheet," World Health Organization, 2014, https://bit.ly/3ohIerK; "World Report on Violence and Health: Summary," World Health Organization, 2002, https://bit.ly/37rFlOe

42   Campbell, Jacqueline et al., "Risk Factors for Femicide in Abusive Relationships: Results from a multisite case control study," *American Journal of Public Health*, July, 2003, available at US National Library of Medicine National Institutes of Health, https://bit.ly/2VukxzS

43   Ibid; Truman, Jennifer L. and Morgan, Rachel E., "Nonfatal Domestic Violence 2003–2012," U.S. Department of Justice, Office of Justice Programs, Bureau of Statistics, April, 2014, https://bit.ly/2JuB98b

44   Dash, Jatinda, "India's Abused Women Break Their Silence Using ATM-type Kiosks," Reuters, November 4, 2014, https://reut.rs/2Vrcio6

45   Ibid.

46   Ibid.

47   "Interviewing Techniques in Domestic Violence Cases Module 4 In-Service Training for Police Officers Student Manual," New Jersey Division of Criminal Justice, revised May, 2003, https://bit.ly/3mBoyhO

48   Jackman, Tom, "Virginia Eliminates Backlog of 2,665 Untested Rape Kits," The *Washington Post*, July 8, 2020, https://wapo.st/3qtNqL5

49   Ibid.

50   Ibid.

51   Ibid.

52   Paresky, Pamlea, "What's Wrong with Locker Room Talk?" *Psychology Today*, October 10, 2016, https://bit.ly/3fZYI4I

53   Ibid.

54   Wiedmann, Corrie, "5 Ways to Get Boys Talking About Feelings and Emotions," Scary Mommy, April 15, 2018, https://bit.ly/39zPQBD

55   "16 Days of Activism Against Gender-Based Violence," UN Women, 2019, https://bit.ly/2KQd1NF

56   Netizens, https://www.netizensfilm.com/

57  Fixtheglitch.org

58  Plank, Liz, "Why the Patriarchy is Killing Men," *The Washington Post*, September 13, 2019, https://wapo.st/33D6yMz

59  Ibid.

60  Qasim, Farwah and Vemuru, Varalakshmi, "Examining the Relationship Between Women's Empowerment and Gender-based Violence: The case of the Nigeria For Women Project," The World Bank, May 13, 2019, https://bit.ly/2VqB1ZJ

61  Ibid.

62  Ibid.

63  HeForShe website, https://www.heforshe.org/en

64  "Facts About Sexual Harassment," US Equal Employment Opportunity Commission, January 15, 1997, https://bit.ly/37wssT1

65  Shaw, Elyse et al., "Sexual Harassment and Assault at Work: Understanding the costs," Institute for Women's Policy Research, October 15, 2018, https://bit.ly/3qjqTQN

66  Feldblum, Chai R. and Lipnic, Victoria A., "Select Task Force on the Study of Harassment in the Workplace," US Equal Employment Opportunity Commission, June 2016, https://bit.ly/2VreITI

67  Ibid.

68  Ibid.

69  Ibid.

70  North, Anna, "7 Positive Changes that Have Come from the #MeToo Movement," Vox, October 4, 2019, https://bit.ly/3lyTdek

71  Feldblum, Chai R. and Lipnic, Victoria A., "Select Task Force on the Study of Harassment in the Workplace," US Equal Employment Opportunity Commission, June 2016, https://bit.ly/2VreITI

72  Rizzo, A. Theodore et al., "The Cost of Sex-Based Harassment to Businesses: An in-depth
    look at the workplace," International Center for Research on Women, 2018, https://bit.ly/36uzLLu

73  Ibid.

74  Ibid.

75  The Restaurant Opportunities Centers United, Forward Together et al., "The Glass Floor: Sexual harassment in the restaurant industry," The Restaurant Opportunities Centers United, October 7, 2014, https://bit.ly/3g2vq5j

76  Liszt, Jeff and Martin, Luke, "Change to Win Letter," Change to Win, May 19, 2020, https://bit.ly/3mzy3Ou.

77  Ibid.

78  Martin, Hugo, "More than 5,000 Hotels Add Security Devices to Protect Workers from Sexual Harassment," *Los Angeles Times*, October 7, 2019, https://lat.ms/3qlsPIt

79  Ibid.

80  "Educating Girls: The path to gender equality," Global Partnership for Education, May, 2019, https://bit.ly/36pAOMK

81  Ibid.

82  "Scope of the Problem: Statistics," RAINN, https://bit.ly/3qnB86z

83  Educating Girls: The path to gender equality," Global Partnership for Education, May, 2019, https://bit.ly/36pAOMK

84  "Haiti: Gender Equality and Women's Empowerment Fact Sheet," USAID, last updated January 10, 2020, https://bit.ly/3olVtHT

85  "Girls More Likely to be Bullied than Boys, English Schools Survey Finds," *The Guardian*, https://bit.ly/3mrHteY

86  Ibid.

87  Ibid.

88  Carroll, Linda, "In Some States, Sexting Could Land Teens in Jail for a Long Time,"

Reuters, April 16, 2019, https://reut.rs/3lxxOlN

89  See "Violence Against Women in Politics: Expert group meeting report and recommendations," UNWomen, March 8-9, 2018, https://bit.ly/39GRkdz

90  "#NotTheCost: Stopping violence against women in politics, Submission by the National Democratic Institute to the United Nations Special Rapporteur on Violence Against Women," National Democratic Institute, June, 2018, https://bit.ly/3oilrMc

91  DiSalvo, Matthew, "In Lead-up to Colombian Elections, Woman Mayoral Candidate is Latest Assassination Victim," The World, September 6, 2019, https://bit.ly/3qjwDKp

92  "Labour MP Jo Cox Dies After Being Shot and Stabbed," The Guardian, https://bit.ly/39zGs0N

93  "Sexism, Harassment, and Violence Against Women Parliamentarians," Inter-Parliamentary Union, October 2016, available at https://bit.ly/2JF190k

94  Ibid.

95  Silverman, Craig, "Alexandria Ocasio-Cortez Hit Back After a GOP Lawmaker Allegedly Called Her a Sexist Slur," Buzzfeed News, July 21, 2020, https://bit.ly/39vrfxU

96  Mauger, Craig, "Detroit Man Arrested After Allegedly Threatening to Kill Whitmer, Nessel," The Detroit News, May 15, 2020, https://bit.ly/36yLOaW

97  Youn, Soo, "Female Public Health Officials say They are 'Shocked' by the Harassment They Face Over Coronavirus Response," The Lily, June 17, 2020, https://bit.ly/37xjR2g

98  Ibid.

99  Oueiss, Ghada, "I'm a Female Journalist in the Middle East. I Won't be Silenced by Online Attacks," The Washington Post, July 8, 2020, https://wapo.st/2JuLiSj

100  Williams, Blair, "A Gendered Media Analysis of the Prime Ministerial Ascension of Gillard and Turnbull: He's 'taken back the reins' and she's 'a backstabbing' murderer," Australian Journal of Political Science, 2017, published online September 11, 2017, https://bit.ly/2I6uxfM

101  "Online Violence: Just because it's viral doesn't make it any less real," Global Fund for Women, https://bit.ly/3fYYSJH

102  Ibid.; Association for Progressive Communications, "Mapping Technology Based Violence Against Women," https://bit.ly/2VzMrud

103  Persaud, Raj and James, David, "Motives Behind Murder of UK Member of Parliament Jo Cox," Psychology Today, June 18, 2016, https://bit.ly/3olpMhB

104  "#NotTheCost: Stopping Violence Against Women in Politics," National Democratic Institute, https://bit.ly/37mbWVm

105  think10.demcloud.org

106  "Bolivia Approves a Landmark Law Against Harassment of Women Political Leaders," UN Women, June 11, 2012, https://bit.ly/2Jz7iv8

107  "Inter-American Model Law on the Prevention, Punishment and Eradication of Violence Against Women in Political Life," Inter-American Commission of Women, Organization of American States, https://bit.ly/3qiQhGq.

108  "Child Marriage," UNICEF Data, April 2020, https://bit.ly/3mDXUVS

109  Ibid.

110  Ibid.

111  "Maternal, Newborn, Child and Adolescent Health: Cause of death among adolescents," World Health Organization Global Health Estimates, 2016, https://bit.ly/2JI11gz

112  Sandstrom, Aleksandra and Theodorou, Angelina E., "Many Countries Allow Child Marriage," Pew Research Center, September 12, 2016, https://pewrsr.ch/3myjniQ

113  Ferguson, Sarah, "What You Need To Know About Child Marriage In The U.S.," Forbes, October 29, 2018, https://bit.ly/2I1dNGz

114  "Chen, Michelle, "About Half of US States Set No Minimum Age for Marriage," The Nation, November 2, 2017, https://bit.ly/3g0HRyy

115  Harmon, Amy and Blinder, Alan, "Delaware Has Banned Marriage Under Age 18.

Other States Also Consider Limits," *The New York Times*, May 17, 2018, https://nyti.ms/37rcOrT. This data was collected from 41 states.

116 Will, K. Sophie, "Why Only Two States Ban Marriage for People Under 18 Years Old," *Deseret News*, October 15, 2018, https://bit.ly/2I1SAwe

117 Sagapolutele, Fili, "Bill Raising the Marriage Age for Girls is Signed into Law," *Samoa News*, September 12, 2018, https://bit.ly/37ztUUO

118 Feleke, Bethlehem, "Delaware Becomes First US State to Fully Ban Child Marriage," CNN, May 12, 2018, https://cnn.it/37veJf4; Livio, Susan K, "New Jersey Bans Child Marriages. New Law Raises Minimum Age to 18," NJ.com, January 20, 2019, https://bit.ly/3lwSVEQ

119 "Mozambique: Assembly Votes to Criminalise Child Marriage," allAfrica Global Media, July 16, 2019, https://bit.ly/3qtYszZ

120 Ibid.

121 Toby, Hellen, "South Sudan Court Rules Against Marriage of Girl,16, in Landmark Case," Thomson Reuters Foundation News, July 9, 2019, https://tmsnrt.rs/39CdcGD

122 "Female Genital Mutilation," World Health Organization, February 3, 2020, https://bit.ly/3gcU8Ap

123 "Female Genital Mutilation or Cutting," US Department of Health and Human Services, Office of Women's Health, April 1, 2019, https://bit.ly/36x2Aa9. The age varies from country to country and even within communities. In about half of the countries, girls are cut before 5 years old. In other countries, most girls are cut between 5 and 14. Sometimes, FGM/C is done to adult women. Women may be cut just before marriage. Some communities wait until the first pregnancy.

124 "Female Genital Mutilation," World Health Organization Human Reproduction Programme, https://bit.ly/3ofiBHU

125 "Female Genital Mutilation or Cutting," US Department of Health and Human Services, Office of Women's Health, April 1, 2019, https://bit.ly/36x2Aa9

126 Ibid.

127 Ibid.

128 "Health Risks of Female Genital Mutilation (FGM)," World Health Organization, https://bit.ly/2I3f0xh

129 Ibid.

130 Varol, Nesrin et al., "Obstetric Outcomes for Women with Female Genital Mutilation at an Australian Hospital, 2006-2012: A descriptive study." *BMC Pregnancy and Childbirth*, 16: 328, 2016, found at https://bit.ly/37vg3i2

131 Van Rossem, R., Meekers, D. "The Decline of FGM in Egypt Since 1987: A cohort analysis of the Egypt Demographic and Health Surveys," *BMC Women's Health*, 20 (100) found at https://bit.ly/3g8vr88

132 Feldman-Jacobs, Charlotte et al., "Abandoning Female Genital Mutilation/Cutting: An in-depth look at promising practices," Population Reference Bureau, December 2006, https://bit.ly/3g2S2mr

133 "21 Million People are Now Victims of Forced Labor, ILO Says," International Labor Organization, June 1, 2012, https://bit.ly/3g1hWH1

134 "What is Human Trafficking?" US Department on Health and Human Services, Office on Trafficking in Persons, last reviewed February 6, 2020, https://bit.ly/2VGLH6Z

135 Ibid.

136 "What is Trafficking in Persons?" US Department of Defense, Combating Trafficking in Persons, https://bit.ly/36BL8lb

137 Ibid.

138 Ibid.

139 Ibid.

140 "What is Modern Slavery?" US Department of State, Office to Monitor and Combat

Trafficking in Persons, https://bit.ly/3fZijC2

141 Ibid.
142 Ibid.
143 Ibid.
144 Ibid.
145 Ibid.
146 Ibid.
147 Ibid.
148 Ibid.
149 Ibid.
150 Ibid.
151 Ibid.
152 See for example, CA SB 657, California legislation that makes human-trafficking disclosure mandatory for all companies in that state. Under this rule, businesses must disclose their own audit efforts and obtain certification from all direct suppliers. The U.K. Modern Slavery Act provides that any company doing business in the U.K. should adhere to these standards, which cover the penalties and enforcement efforts that the government can use to fight trafficking. Subjects can face travel restrictions for up to five years and be forced to disclose information under risk and prevention orders.
153 Nielsen Global, "Consumer-goods' Brands that Demonstrate Commitment to Sustainability Outperform Those That Don't," October 12, 2015, https://bit.ly/3qorDEv
154 https://www.endslaverynow.org/act/buy-slave-free
155 Uribe, Mónica Ortiz, "Activists Decry Femicides After Another Woman Is Killed In Juárez, Mexico," National Public Radio, January 26, 2020, https://n.pr/2KQyAh5
156 https://giwps.georgetown.edu/usa-index/
157 Seager, Joni, "The Women's Atlas," Penguin Books, October 30, 2018, https://bit.ly/37FmD5V
158 http://www.womanstats.org/

CHAPTER FIVE

# See Jane Run

*Instructions for Building Democracy. Step One: Empower Women.*
Madeleine Albright

*If you want a speech to be made, ask a man. If you want anything done, ask a woman.*
Margaret Thatcher

The political empowerment of women is one of the defining characteristics of the modern era. The full and equitable participation of women in public life is essential to building and sustaining strong, vibrant democracies.[1] Increased women's participation results in tangible gains, including governments that are more responsive to citizen needs, increased cooperation across party and ethnic lines, and a more secure and sustainable future for all citizens, regardless of their gender.

At every level, we must engage and value women, from all types of backgrounds and from all walks of life, as voters, as candidates, and as elected or appointed officials. No country can develop effective public policy, legislation, or programs and services without understanding and considering the different needs and life experiences of women and men, whether in terms of access to credit or access to health care.

In the 20th century, women fought for and gained the right to vote in the U.S. and across the globe. One hundred years after the passage of the 19th Amendment – which guaranteed and protected a woman's constitutional right to vote in the U.S. – women are running for office and leading movements for change, challenging the status quo, corruption, and inequality in the U.S. and in places as diverse as China, Chile, Iraq, Kenya, Lebanon, and Hong Kong.

These women, and thousands like them, are taking on diverse and important battles to reform law and policy around domestic violence, inheritance rights, climate change, the way we talk about ourselves, and the ability to pray in the same places as men do.[2] **We need women's voices everywhere.**

Former German Chancellor Angela Merkel (left) with New Zealand's Prime Minister Jacinda Ardern in the forecourt of the Federal Chancellery, Berlin, April 2018.

As elected and appointed officials, and as candidates, women are using their political power to raise critical policy issues, challenge the political establishment and entrenched political order, and bring fresh perspectives to policy debates. In the response to the COVID-19 pandemic, women leaders such as former **German Chancellor Angela Merkel, New Zealand's Prime Minister Jacinda Ardern**, and **Taiwanese President Tsai Ing-wen** have all been praised for steady and decisive responses.

And yet, **women are still vastly underrepresented in public life**. Women now hold only 26.4% of seats in the U.S. Congress and national legislatures around the world, an increase from 12% just 20 years ago.[4] But, this is changing. Nevada is the first state in the U.S. where over half of the legislators are women. In 2021, Nevada's legislature will be 60.3% women,[5, 6] and over half of the legislators in the Colorado House, the New Mexico House, the Oregon House, and the Rhode Island Senate are women.[7] Overall, women will hold more than 30% of seats in state legislatures for the first time in U.S. history.[8] Beginning in 2021, all five members of the Los Angeles County Board of Supervisors will be women. This board is considered the most powerful local government body in the country.[9]

Despite these record numbers, at the current pace, it will take 145.5 years globally for women and men to achieve equal representation in political offices.[10, 11] COVID has had a negative impact on these numbers. Before the pandemic, estimates were that it would take 99.5 years to close the global gender gap in politics. In the U.S., it will take at least 60 years for women to achieve equal representation.[12]

**Women were significantly underrepresented in the initial official U.S. coronavirus response in 2020,[12] but this is changing**. In November 2020, President-elect Biden announced a Coronavirus Task Force, and 38% of its members are women. The members include task force co-chair **Dr. Marcella Nunez-Smith**, the associate dean for health equity research at the Yale School of Medicine, **Dr. Luciana Borio**, Vice President of In-Q-Tel, and senior fellow for global health at the Council on Foreign Relations, **Dr. Celine Gounder**, a clinical assistant professor at the NYU Grossman School of Medicine, **Dr. Julie Morita**, Executive Vice President of the Robert Wood Johnson Foundation, and **Loyce Pace**, the executive director and president of the Global Health Council.[14]

It is critical that women are engaged in this process to ensure that response-and-recovery decisions addressing the pandemic take into account the differential impact of COVID-19 on women and men.

## WOMEN: A POSITIVE IMPACT ON PUBLIC POLICY

When women are part of peace negotiations, for example, agreements that come from these negotiations are more likely to succeed and last between 2 and 15 years longer than if women are not involved.[15] This is critical as most peace agreements fail within five years.[16]

Here are some other critical impacts of having more women in elected and appointed office.

**1. Women in elected office raise different issues and have different perspectives** than their male colleagues. They raise not only issues of women's rights and equal opportunity, but issues faced by their communities, from transportation to healthcare to student loan debt. Importantly, women bring their life experiences and perspectives to policy debates. Issues that appear "gender-neutral" on the surface are almost certainly never gender-neutral.

In Nevada, the state with a majority of women lawmakers, the legislature strengthened domestic-violence laws,[17] added permanent funding to test rape kits,[18] and eliminated the requirement that doctors ask a woman seeking an abortion if she is married.[19]

---

# SNOWPLOWS AND PUBLIC TRANSPORT

Rain and snow do not discriminate, but how cities prioritize the clearance of roads after a snow storm has a gender dimension. In most places, cities plow major roads first, leaving residential streets, sidewalks, and school zones until last. In contrast, Stockholm has a **gender-equal plowing strategy**, clearing sidewalks, bike paths, bus lanes, and daycare zones first, given that women, children, and seniors are more likely to walk, bike, or use mass transit to get to where they need to go.[20]

**Women use public transportation differently than men.**[21] In addition to working outside the home, women have family responsibilities, run more household errands, and maintain family and community ties.[22] Women often "chain" activities, combining multiple stops and destinations within a single trip.[23] This can make public transportation costly, since the traveler may have to pay for numerous single-fare, one-way tickets. There are also challenges if buses aren't on time or aren't easy to use. Finally, routes outside central commuter corridors may not have regular service during off-peak hours, when women are most likely to need public transport for caregiving. Policies need to address these gendered differences.[24]

We know that women have different health care needs because they give birth — and men do not — and because they are most often the primary caregivers for children. Policies that do not take these differences into account will be flawed and ultimately less effective.

**2. More women in elected office means an increase in policies that emphasize quality of life and social protections.**[25] More women legislators translates to a higher priority on health-care access, an increase in social-policy spending, and a decrease in poverty. Countries with more women legislators have higher rates of childhood immunizations and infant- and child-survival rates,[26] spend more on education as a percentage of GDP, and per capita[27] are more likely to ratify environmental treaties,[28] and pass laws that empower women.

**3.** As policymakers, **women use their own life experiences** to identify needs for reform and to create new laws. In 2019, women in the Middle East and North Africa led campaigns to reform laws that dictated a woman could only inherit half of what a man could inherit,[29] and changed laws that restricted a woman's ability to pass her citizenship to a spouse from a different country, or to children she has with that spouse. Here are some other country-specific examples:

- **India** amended its constitution in 1993 to increase the number of women serving on elected local councils (called *panchayats*) to 33% and to ensure that 33% of these councils were chaired by a woman. Across the country, Indian women were most likely to complain to local councils about access to water, regardless of the sex of the person chairing the local council. However, the number of drinking-water projects funded was over 60% higher in women-led councils.[30]
- In **Norway**, researchers found a direct causal relationship between the number of city council seats held by women and the passage of legislation increasing the level of childcare services provided to families by Norwegian municipalities.[31]
- In the **U.S.**, women state legislators are more likely to support gun control, expansion of a social safety net, civil rights, environmental protection, and policies and laws promoting public health and safety. They are also more likely than men to support access to reproductive health services, and the Equal Rights Amendment to the U.S. Constitution.[32]

**4. Women legislators are more responsive to their constituents.** In the U.S., women legislators are more likely to engage in constituent service, and women state legislators report receiving significantly more requests for constituency casework than their male colleagues.[33]

**5. Women's leadership styles are more collaborative.** A study of U.S. state legislators found that women committee chairs resolve conflict by working in a less hierarchical, more participatory, and more collaborative manner.[34] In the U.S. House of Representatives, **Reps. Elissa Slotkin (D–MI)** and **Elise Stefanik (R–NY)** co-sponsored 85 bills in the 116th Congress on a number of key issues.[35] There are similar data globally. Women legislators report they bring a higher level of civility to politics and policymaking than their male colleagues do, and they believe their presence makes a difference in this regard.[36]

## QUESTIONING WOMEN'S APPEARANCE

In politics, women's fashion choices are judged more harshly than their male counterparts. As former Senator Carol Moseley-Braun (D-IL) said, women in politics "are held to a different standard across the board" when it comes to what they wear. Moseley-Braun was criticized for wearing her hair in braids. **Comments about clothing worn by women elected officials** began with Congresswoman Jeannette Rankin, the first woman elected to the House of Representatives, in 1916. A contemporaneous *Washington Post* headline read: "Congresswoman Rankin Real Girl; Likes Nice Gowns and Tidy Hair."[37] In 1993, women in Congress were finally permitted to wear pants, after Senators Barbara A. Mikulski (D-MD) and Nancy Kassebaum (R-KS) did so, and encouraged others to do the same.[38]

## ADVOCACY AND ACTION: WHAT'S THE FIRST STEP?

In Chapter One, I identified a **framework for advocacy and taking action**. Let's use that framework in terms of advocacy and organizing for women's political engagement.

### 1. Identify An Issue You Care About

The general focus for this chapter is electing more women to political office so that governments can more accurately reflect the gender diversity of their constituents and so that policy and spending decisions reflect a broader and more diverse set of perspectives and experiences. You might choose to **narrow this focus** and, for instance, address violence directed at women running for office, or work to change how the media portrays women candidates and elected officials. Narrowing your focus sharpens your goals and makes the rest of the work easier to accomplish and act upon.

### 2. Research: Do Current Laws or Programs Disadvantage Women?

Once you have a focus, then find out if there are laws or policies that impede a woman's ability to run for office, or how women are portrayed when they are running for, or serving in, office. **Are there roadblocks you can help dismantle?**

### 3. Investigate the Context So You Can Understand the Landscape

While every country is different, we know that women's engagement in politics leads to sustainable and effective public policies and programs and more responsive constituent service. Are there policies that can help encourage women to run for office, compete effectively, and serve without being attacked, both literally and in the media? (See **Diving Deep, later in the chapter,** for some examples.)

### 4. Find Out Who Has the Power to Make Change

Let's say you want to focus on the need to address negative and demeaning stereotypes perpetuated by media outlets and commentators about women who are in office. **Create a power map** (see Chapter 1, Step 4) to figure out who has power to deal with that issue. It could be the person who owns or runs a media company, or a media network, or a policy maker who has oversight of media stations at the federal level. It could also be an on-air personality, celebrity or influencer who is also outraged about the treatment of women in politics and wants to take action. In all likelihood, it's a combination of these people and institutions.

**5. Define Your Interest in This Issue**

Once you have identified your issue, and know who has the power to make the necessary changes, it is important to communicate to the person you will be talking to **why this issue is important enough to trigger your actions**. Be clear, concise/short, concrete/understandable, and convincing. (See Chapter 1, Step 5.)

**6. Prepare Your Questions**

Before you ask those in power about **negative media stereotypes of women**, be prepared to make the case that these portrayals inhibit women from running for office.

- Point out that **media** – including newspapers, television, radio, social media, and film – **shapes our values** and cultural and gender norms. Its impact starts to influence people at a young age. These days, children and teens (from ages 8 to 18) engage with the media for over seven hours a day.[39]
- Research shows that – across countries and political systems – **the higher the level of "media sexism," the fewer women run for office**.[40] Studies show a significant relationship between media sexism (measured as the share of all news subjects that are women, and the share of all experts who are women) and the number of women candidates for legislative office.[41]
- **Men still dominate** in every aspect of news, entertainment, and digital media, and coverage is often biased against women.[42] In foreign policy and national security, conversations are overwhelmingly dominated by men. According to Media Matters and Foreign Policy Interrupted,[43] in 2016 women accounted for only 24% of guests featured during news coverage of foreign affairs and national security on major shows. Further, 83% of film and TV narrators are male.[44] Media often puts forward disparaging portrayals of women and girls, sending messages that a woman's value is based on youth, beauty, and sexuality, not her intelligence and capacity as a leader. Male characters dominate entertainment media, with a ratio of approximately three to one male characters to female characters.
- Review the information in **Diving Deep** (below).
- Review the material suggested in the **Resources** section of this chapter (remember: INFORMATION IS POWER!).

---

## THE LEADERSHIP GENDER GAP STARTS EARLY

For example, while 56% of college students are women,[45] only 40% of college student-body presidents are women.[46] Closing this gap is important to increase the number of women interested in running for political office and other leadership roles. Women who served as student-body presidents are 11% more likely to run for political office.[47] 40% of women serving in the U.S. Congress were involved in student government.[48] *Ask what your company/organization is doing to encourage young women to assume leadership roles.*

**Here are some questions to ask media executives:**

- How many women political reporters do you have (what percentage of your political reporters are women)?
- How many women editors for political stories (what percentage of the political editors are women)?
- How many women are on-air personalities for major, prime-time news shows (what percentage of on-air personalities for those shows are women)?
- Do you track political coverage and what is said about candidates? Do you break down this information by the sex of the candidates?
- Do you have a process or an ombudsman to deal with complaints about media bias against women candidates or office holders?

## THE POWER OF TV TO LEAD SOCIAL CHANGE

The media can be a positive force in challenging norms and stereotypes as well. The show *Will and Grace* is widely credited with increasing support for gay rights.[49] Storylines on *ER* that dealt with teen obesity, hypertension, and healthy eating habits had a positive impact on the attitudes and behaviors of viewers, particularly men.[50] A 2018 analysis of the leading characters in the 50 most popular children's TV programs found that women accounted for 52% of the lead or co-lead roles, and that speaking time during those shows had also reached or exceeded equality.[51]

### 7. Develop Suggestions for Solving the Challenges You Are Raising

It's important to suggest solutions for the issue you are raising. If you don't, those with power may dismiss you and question your commitment. **The solution you propose doesn't have to be perfect, or solve the entire problem.** But putting *something* forward reflects your seriousness and interest in making change. It also gives your effort more focus, which makes it easier for others to organize around it and thus amplify your message. Here are some ideas to get you going:

- If you are concerned about **money in politics and its impact on women's ability to compete as candidates**, organize to support spending and fundraising caps. Washington, D.C., has a voluntary public-financing program,[52] with caps on the amount a candidate can spend (from $1,000 to $40,000) and caps on individual donations to campaigns (from $20 to $200, depending on the office). This type of program makes running for office less expensive and less onerous in terms of fundraising.
- If you are concerned that there are **not enough women staff working for elected officials**, use existing databases to create a baseline from which to make that claim, such as the Congressional Leadership Directories (also known as the Yellow Books).[53] In a study using 2016 data, the *Washington Post* found that women in Congressional staff jobs had predominantly administrative and constituent-service responsibilities, and women were less likely to be legislative assistants, legislative correspondents, and legislative counsels.[54] If you can't find the data you want, create that database yourself.

Either way, use the data to ask questions. For example, using publicly available data from the U.S. Senate Foreign Relations Committee and the U.S. House Foreign Affairs Committee, I co-authored a piece about the lack of women experts testifying before Congressional committees tasked with foreign policy and national security.[55]

## 8. Ask Your Questions and Outline Your Suggestions

There are many ways to ask the questions you've developed, and you should use the combination that works for you. You can:

- Send a letter or email.
- Engage on social media about your issue with others who share your views, and/or with decision-makers.
- Ask in person at meetings or if you see the policy maker in person at an event.
- Make an appointment specifically to talk about the issue, ask your questions, and if appropriate be ready with a concrete ask for the meeting. For example, you can ask the person you are meeting with if they will consider a policy change or sponsor relevant legislation (if needed), or ask if they will commit to looking into the issue and consider your suggestion for action on the issue. Or at the very least, ask them if you can return for another meeting in a month to discuss progress.

If you need a script for your conversation, here's a start. You should only address one issue in each phone call, video chat, or letter:

*Hello, my name is _____, and I am a constituent of President/Governor/Senator _____. I am calling/writing to urge that Senator ____ vote yes (or no) on bill number ____ about addressing violence against women in politics. Do you know how she will vote?*

Asking questions forces these institutions to gather data in order to answer you. Absent a question, people may not know that certain policies and practices are discriminatory. A political party may be fielding a large number of women candidates, but these candidates may disproportionately be running in districts where they are unlikely to win. An elected official may have a large number of women on staff, but he or she may not know that women are in lower-ranking positions or paid less than men in similar positions.[56]

Making a suggestion demonstrates your commitment to the issue, and if you've done your homework, the person you are meeting with will at least consider following through on your ideas *in some way*, or will open up a dialog about how to move forward in another way.

## 9. What's Next? Follow up!

Once you have taken all of these steps, keep the pressure on decision-makers so that your issue isn't forgotten. In other words, following up is important. This means:

- **MOST IMPORTANT:** Send a thank-you note. In most cases you will want to include a recap of what was discussed.
- Consider working with an "organizing and advocacy partner." This can be a friend or family member who can serve as a sounding board and a

collaborator as you strategize and move forward.

- More than likely there will be a number of actions you can take after your initial meeting. Work with your advocacy partner or with the organization you are working with on the issue to come up with a plan of action.
- Ask for another meeting (remember to get to know the staff who support the decision-maker as they can be helpful in getting that next meeting).
- Monitor the issue and your progress.
- Identify and engage with other individuals who are interested in the issue. **Start to organize them to take action.**
- Identify and engage with those who can influence the relevant decision-makers on your issue.
- Develop a tracking system if you are trying to get legislation introduced or a policy changed. Include names and pertinent information on:
  - Legislators who are co-sponsors
  - Decision-makers who can change policy
  - Legislators who (and how many) support you
  - Legislators who (and how many) oppose you (this last item is particularly important!)

## TAKE ACTION IN YOUR DAILY LIFE!

You may decide that the most important thing you can do is **raise awareness at home.** If that is the case, then you can engage people at the grassroots and make the case that people in your community should care about **electing more women to political office – locally, in your state, and nationwide.**

### 1. Register to vote, and vote.

Women must exercise this hard-won right, which became a Constitutional right only in 1920, after 70 years of struggle. Motivating more women to vote is critical to ensure their voices are heard. While more women than men vote today in the United States,[57] 53% of "chronic nonvoters" are women.[58]

An effective project to motivate women-of-color voters was created by **Moms-Rising**. In the 2018 midterm election, women reached by the group's **Be a Voter, Raise a Voter** program turned out at rates 13% higher than the average for moms of color in Florida, and 11% better in North Carolina. As part of the effort, Moms-Rising provided games and art projects at polling places so moms could take their kids with them to vote. The group also encouraged members to send out texts and handwritten postcards urging others to vote.[59]

Another example of creative engagement is **VotER**, a voter-registration campaign started by Dr. Alister Martin, an emergency-room doctor at Massachusetts General Hospital. VotER provides patients, visitors, and staff with the opportunity to register to vote, or check to see if they are registered to vote, right at the hospital.[60]

### 2. Join efforts to get out the vote (GOTV)

You can make phone calls, write postcards, send emails and texts, and/or go door-to-door (once it is safe!) to talk to voters. Many people don't like GOTV activities as they are worried about being provoked into arguments. Know that most often, as

## WOMEN'S SUFFRAGE AND THE 19th AMENDMENT

American women did not always have the right to vote. Women fought for 70 years for and finally gained this right in 1920 when the **19th Amendment to the Constitution** was ratified. Despite the 19th Amendment, in practice many non-White women couldn't vote due to literacy tests, poll taxes, and violence.[61] Further, many Native American and Asian American women did not gain the right to vote until much later, as they did not hold U.S. citizenship. [62]

The women activists who fought for the right to vote pioneered techniques that are still used today: they marched, went to prison, chained themselves to The White House, lobbied office holders and candidates at every level and in both political parties, and navigated complex political and legal terrain. They organized across the country – riding trains, sending telegrams – with no access to social media and cell phones. From the time of the first bitter referendum in 1867 to ratification of the 19th Amendment, the suffragists undertook 480 petition and lobbying drives to convince state legislatures to submit suffrage amendments to voters, organized 277 campaigns to get state party conventions to include women's suffrage in their platforms, and conducted 56 state-referendum campaigns.[63]

elections approach, when you do GOTV you are assigned to talk only with voters who already support your candidate, party, or cause, or could probably be convinced to do so.

These efforts are critical as **every vote counts**. Here are examples of elections that were decided by a handful of votes, or in some cases, a coin toss.

- 2020: In Iowa, a race for the U.S. House of Representatives was decided by six votes.[64]

- 2018: In Maryland, the Democratic primary for Baltimore County Executive was decided by 17 votes.[65]

- 2017: In Virginia, a race for the House of Delegates ended in a tie after more than 23,000 votes were cast. The tie was broken by pulling a name out of a bowl, and Republican David Yancey was declared the winner. This had statewide impact as his win gave Republicans control of Virginia's House of Delegates by one seat. *An important update* to this story is that in 2019, Delegate Yancey was defeated by his 2017 opponent, Shelly Simonds, who received almost 58% of the vote.[66]

- 2016: In New Mexico, a state House seat was decided by two votes out of 14,000.[67]

### 3. Run for office yourself and/or support other women who run.

An astonishing six women ran for the Democratic Party nomination for President of the United States in 2020,[68] the same year record numbers of women ran for office in the U.S.: 583 women ran for the U.S. House (356 Democrats and 227 Republicans) and 60 women ran for the U.S. Senate (37 Democrats and 23 Republicans).[69]

Compare that to the 2016 cycle, when only 212 women ran for the House and 25 for the Senate.[70] We see increased activism and interest by women across the country. In 2020, this increase in the number of women running for Congress has continued,[71] such that women comprise 28% of candidates filing.

Despite these numbers, **women are still less likely to run for office than men**.[72] Women and men in business, law, education, and politics/activism – fields that tend to generate candidates – have virtually the same relevant experience (policy expertise and analysis, public speaking, and fundraising). But when asked if they were qualified to run for office, only 57% of women said they were qualified, compared to 73% of men.[73]

Also, women who lose an election are less likely to run a second time. According to a study of 11,000 candidates who ran in local California elections, women who lost were *half as likely* to try again than men. The study concluded that if these women ran again, and won at the same rate as others in the same situation, the number of women in office would increase by 17%.[74]

If you are thinking about running, there are many groups that help women candidates develop confidence and needed skills. Some work only with candidates from a particular political party; some are nonpartisan. (See **Resources** for a list of some of these groups.) If you aren't running for office now, make sure to support other women running who share your values. You can volunteer on their campaigns and raise money for them. You can activate your networks to support your own candidacy or those of other women.

**4. Express your opinion by using media platforms.**

It is important to be part of discussions and debates in both traditional and social media. This can include writing letters to the editor, blogging, and calling into local talk radio. Letters to the editor are especially effective because they reach a large audience, are often monitored by elected officials, and can add additional information and views not addressed in a news article. Effective letters to the editor are short and address one subject or article. Emphasize your view in the first sentence, such as, "I am deeply saddened to read that Congressman Doe is working to roll back affirmative action. (*Title of Article*, date)."

Blogs can also reach large audiences, and they allow you to address a topic in a more in-depth manner than a letter to the editor. But keep your blog entries short (500 to 600 words) so that readers don't lose interest.

Whether you are writing a letter to the editor, blogging, or posting on Instagram, Facebook, or any other social medium, you can do this on your own, or organize a group to read articles and papers and decide which are worth a response. This is a good task to organize your friends and networks around.

## SUMMARY

This chapter outlines how women's access to politics and power is limited in many places, how electoral systems, laws, and gender norms create barriers, and how communities and countries benefit when more and more women are elected to public office.

In addition to the **Framework for Advocacy and Action**, which offers detailed information about how you can effectively advocate for increased access to political participation and civic engagement for women, **Take Action at Home** has some concrete suggestions about how to engage friends and family on the grassroots level in an effort to convince them of the importance of electing more women at every level of government.

# ROLE MODELS AND TRAILBLAZERS

Agree with these women politically or not, they have each broken a barrier for women in U.S. politics.

**Victoria Woodhull** ran for President about 50 years before women had the right to vote. Her 1872 campaign platform, under the banner of the Equal Rights Party, focused on women's rights and sexual freedom.[75] A maverick, Woodhull was also the first woman to address a Congressional committee, own a brokerage firm in New York City, and start a newspaper.[76]

**Congresswoman Shirley Chisholm** was the first Black woman to serve as a U.S. Representative, elected in 1968 by the voters of New York's 12th Congressional District. In 1972 she campaigned as the first major-party Black candidate for President, running as a Democrat. (Senator Margaret Chase Smith had run as a Republican in 1964).[76]

**Secretary Hillary Rodham Clinton** has had many titles. She was a staff member on the House Judiciary Committee during the Nixon impeachment inquiry, law firm partner, First Lady of Arkansas, First Lady of the United States; first woman to serve as U.S. Senator from New York, U.S. Secretary of State; 2016 Democratic nominee for President and the first woman to be nominated from a major political party. She is also the author of eight books.[78]

**Speaker Nancy Pelosi** is the first woman Speaker of the U.S. House of Representatives, and as Speaker, is third in line to succeed the President should he or she be unable to serve. She previously served as the chair of the California Democratic Party, and finance chair of the Democratic Senatorial Campaign Committee. She has been a Member of Congress since 1985.[79]

**Congresswoman Geraldine Ferraro** became the first woman nominated as the vice-presidential candidate on a major party ticket in 1984. She began her career as a prosecutor and served as a Democratic Member of Congress from New York from 1979 to 1985.[80]

**Senator Margaret Chase Smith** was the first woman to win election to both the U.S. House and the U.S. Senate. She was a Republican, but cultivated a career as an independent legislator, speaking out against McCarthyism. At the 1964 Republican Convention she became the first woman to have her name put in for nomination for the presidency by a major political party.[81]

**Congresswoman Jeannette Rankin** was the first woman elected to Congress, one of the few suffragists elected to Congress, and the only Member of Congress to vote against U.S. participation in both World War I and World War II. "I may be the first woman member of Congress," she observed upon her election in 1916. "But I won't be the last."[82]

**Governor Sarah Palin** became Alaska's youngest and first woman governor in 2006. Two years later she was tapped as Republican presidential nominee John McCain's running mate, making her the first woman in her party to run for vice president. After resigning as Alaska governor in 2009, Palin went on to serve as a contributor for Fox News.[83]

**Senator Barbara A. Mikulski** was the first Democratic woman elected to the U.S. Senate in her own right in 1986, and when she retired in 2016 was the longest serving woman in the U.S. Congress. She was also the first woman to chair the powerful Senate Committee on Appropriations. Widely considered the "Dean of

Clockwise from upper left: Victoria Woodhull; Poster from Shirley Chisholm's 1972 Presidential Campaign, Secretary Hillary Rodham Clinton, House Speaker Nancy Pelosi, Representative Geraldine Ferraro, Senator Margaret Chase Smith

Clockwise from upper left: Jeannette Pickering Rankin, the first woman to hold federal office in the U.S. (elected to the House of Representatives in 1916 and again in 1940); former Alaska Governor Sarah Palin campaigns in Iowa; Senator Barbara Mikulski; Vice President Kamala Harris.

the Women Senators," she was a mentor to the other women who were elected to the Senate, and began the tradition of a bipartisan dinner once a month.[84]

**Vice President Kamala Harris** was was sworn in on January 20, 2021. She is the first woman, the first Black person, and the first Asian-American to serve as Vice President. Prior to her election as Vice President, she served in the U.S. Senate representing California from 2017 to 2020. She began her career in the Alameda County District Attorney's Office, and in 2003, she was elected district attorney of San Francisco. She was elected attorney general of California in 2010, and re-elected in 2014. She was the first African-American, the first Asian-American, and the third woman vice presidential running mate on a major party ticket.[85]

Five women have been appointed to the U.S. Supreme Court: Justices **Sandra Day O'Connor, Sonia Sotomayor, Ruth Bader Ginsburg, Elena Kagan** and **Amy Coney Barrett.**

**Sandra Day O'Connor** was the first woman to serve on the U.S. Supreme Court, appointed by President Ronald Reagan in 1981. She graduated third in her class from Stanford Law School, but struggled to find employment in the legal field. She began her legal career working for the county attorney of San Mateo for free, after turning down a paid position as a legal secretary. In 1957 she went into private practice, and then worked as an assistant attorney general of Arizona. Beginning in 1969, O'Connor served in the Arizona State Senate and was the first woman majority leader in any state senate. She was elected to the Superior Court of Maricopa County in 1975, and was appointed to the Arizona Supreme Court of Appeals four years later. She was unanimously confirmed by the Senate.[86]

Before being appointed to the Supreme Court in 1993, **Ruth Bader Ginsburg** was a trailblazing advocate against gender discrimination, successfully arguing six landmark cases before the U.S. Supreme Court. Ginsburg was appointed to the U.S. Court of Appeals for the District of Columbia in 1980 by President Jimmy Carter, and thirteen years later was appointed to the Supreme Court by President Bill Clinton.[87] She died in September 2020, and was the first woman to ever lie in state in the U.S. Capitol.

**Sonia Sotomayor** is the first Hispanic to serve on the U.S. Supreme Court. She began her career as a prosecutor in New York and, after a time in private practice, was nominated to the U.S. District Court for the Southern District of New York. She gained fame as the judge who "saved" Major League Baseball with her decision in *Silverman v. Major League Baseball Player Relations Committee, Inc.* President Bill Clinton nominated Sotomayor to the U.S. Court of Appeals for the Second Circuit in 1997, and in 2009 she was appointed to the Supreme Court by President Barack Obama.[88]

**Elena Kagan** is the only sitting justice with no prior judicial experience. She brings a diverse viewpoint, often using pop culture references in opinions. Kagan was a Supreme Court clerk for Justice Thurgood Marshall, taught law at the University of Chicago Law School and Harvard Law School (where she was the first woman dean), and served in several positions in the Clinton Administration. President Obama nominated her to be Solicitor General (the first woman to hold that position) and in 2009, she was confirmed to the Supreme Court.[89]

**Amy Coney Barrett** was confirmed in October 2020, having previously served as a judge on the United States Court of Appeals for the Seventh Circuit from 2017 to 2020. Before and while serving on the federal bench, she has been a professor of law at Notre Dame Law School, where she has taught civil procedure, constitutional law, and statutory interpretation.[90]

Painting, "The Four Justices," 2012, by Nelson Shanks. National Portrait Gallery. Gift of Ian M. and Annette P. Cumming.

# DIVING DEEP

You've seen the importance of engaging women in the political process at every level of government in order to develop effective public policy, legislation, programs, and services that consider the different needs and life experiences of women as well as men. Here is more in-depth information that you can use as an advocate for why women's engagement is critical.

## ADDRESSING CHALLENGES EMBEDDED IN ELECTORAL SYSTEMS

Women operate in diverse political systems across the globe and in countries at different levels of gender equality in public life. While country contexts are different, many of the structural and normative impediments to women's participation are similar. These impediments include

- The structure of the electoral process and system
- Social norms around the role of women and their participation in politics
- Male-dominated institutions
- Unwelcoming political parties that are resistant to fielding women candidates in winnable positions
- Hostile and belittling media coverage
- Women's time constraints, based on multiple roles
- Electoral violence

### Electoral Systems Matter

While sometimes controversial, **electoral quotas** are the most effective way to increase the number of women in office. There is a quota system in place in almost every country where at least 30% of the members of a national legislature are women.[91] In almost 130 countries, quotas are mandated by the country's constitution and/or electoral laws, or by a political party's governing documents. The most effective quotas have sanctions for noncompliance and include mandates for placing women high on party electoral lists.[92]

Further, more women are elected to public office in the context of electoral systems based on **proportional representation**, where legislative seats are assigned in proportion to the number of votes received by a party. In these systems, political parties have an incentive to run diverse candidates that appeal to a wide range of voters, rather than maximize one individual's chance of winning. On average, eight percent more women are elected in proportional representation systems than in winner-take-all systems, which are the systems currently in place in the U.S. and Canada.[93] Countries with less than 10% of women in their parliament are far more likely to have a winner-take-all system than a proportional one.

New Zealand moved from a winner-take-all to a proportional system in 1990. After that move, the proportion of women in the Parliament grew from 16.5% to 21% in three years, and then to 29% another three years later.[94] Today, New Zealand's Parliament has 41% women and the country has had three women Prime Ministers.[95]

### Political Parties Are the Ultimate Gatekeepers

This is true everywhere. Political parties are gatekeepers to political power and resources, and are overwhelmingly male dominated. It is critical to understand that party leaders make decisions about who the party will support as a candidate, how financial and other resources will be allocated, and what policies are a priority.

Embedded in the way political parties operate are structural barriers that make it harder for women to participate fully in all internal policymaking decisions and candidate selection, and incorporate the issues that women care about in political platforms.

Here are some specific questions you can ask of **political leaders, elected officials**, and their **staff**.

- What is the breakdown (by sex, race, and age) of members in your party leadership?
- Who is the highest-ranking woman in your political party?
- How many women are on your party's decision-making body?
- What have you done to increase the number of women members in your party? The number of young women? The number of women of color?
- Do you have a code of conduct regarding the use of language on social and traditional media?
- How do you deal with party members or candidates who use sexist or racist language?
- Who is the highest-ranking woman on your staff?
- What policies do you champion that help women and/or girls?
- What policies do you or your party promote to reach gender equality?
- Do you provide training to women candidates, elected officials, and staff on how to engage with traditional and social media?

**Madame President or Madame Prime Minister?**

Since 1960, only 73 women have ever served as head of state.[96] As of April 2021, **11 women are serving as heads of state and 12 are serving as heads of government**,[97, 98] (women comprise almost 6% of heads of government and 5% of heads of state). The number of women heads of state has remained relatively low, hovering around 10 to 15 women heads of state at any one time around the globe. Women hold 18% of **ministerial portfolios.**[99]

Women presidents and prime ministers take one of two paths to power: (1) serving as a representative of a deceased (often assassinated) male family member or (2) climbing the ladder of the country's political and party systems. In many cases, the women in the latter category come from politically prominent families.

> # WOMEN OF COLOR IN THE U.S. CONGRESS
>
> 12,415 people have served in Congress since it was created in 1789. Of that number, in the House of Representatives, 83 members have been women of color. In that time, only five women of color have served in the Senate.

## CONFLICT AS CHANGE AGENT

The country with the most women in parliament is Rwanda (over 60%).[102] In Rwanda, 50% of cabinet ministers and 50% of Supreme Court judges are women. The most cited reason for these stunningly high numbers is that the 1994 genocide decimated the population of men. As the country rebuilt post-genocide, gender equality was made a national priority and was established in the country's 2003 constitution.[103]

In fact, researchers have found that conflict can propel larger numbers of women to office. Conflicts can restructure institutions as well as existing gender norms, opening up space for women in government.[104]

**Women are underrepresented in national legislatures.**

Globally, 25% of parliamentarians are women,[100, 101] which translates to over 11,000 women holding seats in national legislatures. Here are the regional statistics on the number of women in parliaments:

- Nordic States: 43.9%
- The Americas: 31.3%
- Europe, overall: 29.9%
- Sub-Saharan Africa: 24.4%
- Asia: 20%
- Pacific: 19.4%
- Middle East and North Africa: 16.6%

### MORE ON THE MEDIA

Unfortunately, as discussed above, the media often puts forward **disparaging portrayals of women and girls**, sending messages that a woman's value is based on youth, beauty, and sexuality, not her intelligence or her capacity as a leader. Male characters dominate entertainment media, with a ratio of approximately three to one male characters to female characters. Further, 83% of film and TV narrators are male.[105]

**Gender pay gaps persist in newsrooms** at major outlets, such as the *Associated Press*, the *Los Angeles Times*, the *New York Times*, the *San Francisco Chronicle*, the *Wall Street Journal*, and the *Washington Post*, with men earning substantially more than women.[106] Wage disparity in media made headlines in 2017 when the British Broadcasting Corporation (BBC) was forced to publish the salaries of those earning more than £150,000 a year, showing for the first time how many men were paid substantially more than similarly situated (and similarly well-known) women.[107]

**BBC update**: The BBC recently launched the 50/50 initiative mandating that every department keep track of the gender balance of journalists and of who is featured and interviewed in stories. The goal is to bring that number to 50/50 by intensive and consistent reporting, including how many women journalists had their work published on BBC.[108]

**In film, gender pay gaps are more glaring.** Although Hollywood's women actors are well-paid compared to most Americans, they make less than their male colleagues.[109] For example, when scenes had to be re-shot for the 2017 film *All the Money in the World*, the two co-stars were treated very differently in terms of pay. Mark Wahlberg was paid $1.5 million for re-shooting his scenes, but co-star Michelle Williams was paid only $1,000.[110] After the pay disparity became public, Wahlberg donated the $1.5 million he received for the re-shoots to the Time's Up Legal Defense Fund.[111]

Women journalists in the U.S. and abroad report that **online harassers** regularly direct lewd comments, sexual solicitations, and rape threats against them.[112] At 14 of the nation's largest newspapers, the number of articles published on sexual assault and harassment surged by 30% during the 15 months after Hollywood mogul Harvey Weinstein's sexual crimes made the news, according to the Women's Media Center.[113]

## WHO REPORTS THE NEWS?

The percentage of White men who work in newsrooms is 77%, which is 12 points higher than the percentage of White men in the overall U.S. workforce, according to the Pew Research Center.[114] The good news: more women than men are studying journalism.[115]

## CONCLUSION

Electing women is the first – but not only – step toward enacting more equitable policies. We also need women and men in political parties and elected offices championing these policies. Closing gender gaps and securing women's safety, well-being, prosperity, and freedom are fundamentally important, as is a gender focus across all issues, from infrastructure to defense policy. Building strong legal frameworks, addressing cultural norms, enabling access to resources and decision-making, and reducing GBV increases everyone's ability to participate fully in their communities.

# RESOURCES: Politics & Public Life
## Information Is Power

In every chapter of the book you will find a list of resources that you can refer to when you are formulating your initial questions, doing your research, finding out who has the power to make change, preparing your questions, and making an advocacy plan. Here you will find resources to help you work to elect more women to political office.

These lists are available/updated at: stepheniefoster.com

## Movies and TV

- **A Woman Called Golda (1982)**. The made-for-television movie starring Ingrid Bergman as Israeli Prime Minister Golda Meir.

- **All In: The Fight for Democracy (2020)**. This film by former Minority Leader of the Georgia House of Representatives Stacey Abrams explores the long-standing issue of voter suppression.

- **Ann (2020)**. A portrait of Governor of Texas Ann Richards (1991-1995), written and starring Holland Taylor. The play earned Taylor a Tony Award nomination for Best Lead Actress in a Play. This production was recorded in Austin, Texas, in 2013 and telecast via PBS' Great Performances.

- **And She Could Be Next (2020)**. Filmed by a team of women filmmakers of color, this two-part documentary focuses on women of color organizing and running for office, including Stacey Abrams (Georgia), Rashida Tlaib (Michigan), Lucy McBath (Georgia), Veronica Escobar (Texas), Maria Elena Durazo (California), and Bushra Amiwala (Illinois). The film was executive produced by Ava DuVernay. **#TralblazersPBS**.

- **God Sleeps in Rwanda (2005)**. Follows five women rebuilding their lives after the 1994 genocide.

- **The Iron Lady (2011)**. Starring Meryl Streep as Margaret Thatcher, this drama is based on the life and career of the first woman Prime Minister of the United Kingdom.

- **Knock Down the House (2019)**. This documentary chronicles the primary campaigns of Alexandria Ocasio-Cortez, Amy Vilela, Cori Bush, and Paula Jean Swearengin, four progressive Democrats who ran for Congress in the 2018 midterm elections.

- **Long Shot (2019)**. A romantic comedy starring Charlize Theron as the U.S. Secretary of State who decides to hire someone she once babysat as her speechwriter when she runs for President. A lighter look at women running for office, this movie touches on the sexism and double standards women face.

- **Miss Representation (2011)**. Written and directed by Jennifer Siebel Newsom, this documentary exposes how mainstream media and culture contribute to the underrepresentation of women in positions of power and influence in America.

- **Mrs. America (2020).** Airing on FX for Hulu, Mrs. America is a miniseries on the fight for the Equal Rights Amendment in 1970s America and the backlash led by conservative activist Phyllis Schlafly. The cast includes Cate Blanchett, Rose Byrne, Uzo Aduba, Elizabeth Banks, Tracey Ullman, and Sarah Paulson.

- **Not for Ourselves Alone: The Story of Elizabeth Cady Stanton and Susan B. Anthony (1999).** PBS: The American Lives Film Project, Inc.

- **Patsy Mink: Ahead of the Majority (2008).** In 1965, Patsy Takemoto Mink was the first Asian-American woman elected to the U.S. Congress. Mink was the driving force behind Title IX, the landmark legislation that transformed women's opportunities in higher education and athletics.

- **She Votes.** The episodes in this podcast examine the complex history of the women's suffrage movement in the U.S. Hosted by award-winning journalists Ellen Goodman and Lynn Sherr.

- **Suffragette (2015).** A British historical drama about the women's suffrage movement in the United Kingdom. Starring Carey Mulligan, Helena Bonham Carter, and Meryl Streep.

- **The Vote (2020).** Airing on PBS in honor of the 100th anniversary of the 19th Amendment, this documentary tells the story of the fight for the right of American women to vote. It includes special sections on the fight for the right to vote for women of color, which took decades longer.

## Books

- *Becoming* (2018) by Michelle Obama. A powerful and inspiring memoir by the former First Lady of the United States.

- *The Breakthrough: Politics and Race in the Age of Obama* (2009) by Gwen Ifill. Veteran journalist Ifill shows how the Black political struggle in the United States in the 1960s gave way to a generation of men and women who are direct beneficiaries of the civil rights movement.

- *Hard Choices: A Memoir* (2014) by Hillary Clinton. An inside account of the crises, challenges, and hard choices Clinton faced during her four years as U.S. Secretary of State, and how those experiences continue to shape her views of the future.

- *Hell and Other Destinations: A 21st-Century Memoir* (2020) by Madeleine Albright. A funny, inspiring, intimate, and detailed memoir by the former U.S. Secretary of State, who continues to command high visibility on the world stage.

- *Jailed for Freedom: American Women Win the Vote* (1920, reissued in 1995) by Doris Stevens. Reissued to commemorate the 75th anniversary of the 19th Amendment to the U.S. Constitution, this commemorative edition was edited by Carol O'Hare to update the book for a more modern audience.

- *Madame President: The Extraordinary Journey of Ellen Johnson-Sirleaf* (2017) by Helene Cooper. The story of Ellen Johnson-Sirleaf, winner of the

Nobel Peace Prize and the first democratically elected woman president in African history.

- *My Beloved World* (2013) by Sonia Sotomayor. A memoir written by the first Hispanic justice on the United States Supreme Court, about her childhood, education, and life through 1992.

- *Our Woman in Havana: A Diplomat's Chronicle of America's Long Struggle with Castro's Cuba* (2018) by Vicki Huddleston. A look at several decades of U.S.-Cuba relations from State Department veteran Vicki Huddleston, the top U.S. diplomat in Havana under Presidents Clinton and George W. Bush.

- *Pelosi* (2020) by Molly Ball. Written by award-winning political journalist Molly Ball, this book is an intimate perspective on one of the most powerful women in American political history, House Speaker Nancy Pelosi.

- *Ruth Bader Ginsburg: A Life* (2018) by Jane Sherron De Hart. This comprehensive, revelatory biography explores the central experiences that crucially shaped Ginsburg's passion for justice, her advocacy for gender equality, and her meticulous jurisprudence. Written by historian De Hart over 15 years with Ginsburg's cooperation, it is based on many interviews with the justice, her husband, her children, her friends, and her associates.

- *Tough Love: My Story of the Things Worth Fighting For* (2019) by Susan Rice. An insider's account on some of the most complex national security, diplomatic, and foreign policy issues over three decades from the perspective of the National Security Advisor to President Obama and U.S. Ambassador to the United Nations.

- *The Woman's Hour* (2018) by Elaine Weiss. The nail-biting climax of one of the greatest political victories in American history: the down-and-dirty campaign to get the last state – Tennessee – to ratify the 19th Amendment to the U.S. Constitution, granting women the right to vote.

## Organizations

### Groups that help elect women Democratic candidates:

- **EMILY's List** supports pro-choice Democratic women running for office at the federal and state level. EMILY's List is one of the most successful PACs and political organizations in the country. www.emilyslist.org

- **Emerge America** works through almost 30 state chapters to recruit, train, and provide a network to Democratic women who want to run for office. Its signature program is an in-depth, six-month, 70-hour training program for candidates. www.emergeamerica.org

### Groups that help elect women Republican candidates:

- **Maverick PAC** is a national network for conservative young business professionals organized to elect Republican candidates for federal office, especially candidates who are millennials. www.maverickpac.com

- **RightNOW Women PAC** contributes to promising Republican women congressional candidates across the country. www.rightnowwomen.org

- **Maggie's List** is focused on electing conservative women to federal public office. www.maggieslist.org

**Nonpartisan groups focused on helping women candidates, regardless of party:**

- The clothing company **M.M.LaFleur** lends clothes to women candidates of any party, whether they are running for town council or Congress. Candidates who contact the company will receive five free outfits selected for them. **#readytorun** https://mmlafleur.com/mdash/ready-to-run-for-office

- **The Campaign School at Yale University** is a nonpartisan, issue-neutral leadership program, with a mission to increase the number and influence of women in elected and appointed offices in the U.S. and globally. www.tcsyale.org

- **Higher Heights For America** is a national membership-based organization dedicated to electing Black women to office. https://www.higherheightsforamerica.org

- **Running Start** is a nonpartisan non-profit that trains young women to run for public office. www.runningstart.org

- **She Should Run** is a nonpartisan organization to inspire women to run for office, with a goal of 250,000 women running for office by 2030. www.sheshouldrun.org

- **Council of Women World Leaders**
Founded in 1996, it is the only organization in the world dedicated to women heads of state and government. The network includes 74 current and former Prime Ministers and Presidents. www.councilwomenworldleaders.org

- **Geena Davis Institute on Gender in Media**
The Institute is the only organization working collaboratively within the entertainment industry to engage and educate, in an effort to create gender balance, foster inclusion, and reduce negative stereotyping in family entertainment media. www.seejane.org

- **League of Women Voters (LWV)**
Founded after women gained the right to vote, the LWV is a nonpartisan, grassroots organization. LWV encourages informed and active participation in government, works to increase understanding of major public-policy issues, and influences public policy through education and advocacy. LWV also registers voters and provides election information through voter guides as well as candidate forums and debates. www.lwv.org

- **National Democratic Institute for International Affairs (NDI)**
Along with its sister organization, the International Republican Institute, NDI promotes democracy globally. NDI's Gender, Women and Democracy program supports women to overcome the barriers to their equal and active political participation. www.ndi.org

- **Supermajority and the Supermajority Education Fund**
Supermajority is building an inclusive, national membership of women who are connected, empowered, and taking action, from increasing their level of civic engagement and advocacy to voting. The Supermajority Education Fund is dedicated to research and education about women's power, awareness, visibility, and civic participation. www.supermajority.com

- **Unbought–Unbossed (UnB2)**
Launched in the summer of 2018 by Kimberly Ellis, UnB2 is an incubator for the next generation of political disruptors. It is focused on civic education, civic engagement, and civic empowerment. It was created to support the work of everyday activists. www.unb2.org

- **Vital Voices Global Partnership**
Vital Voices invests in women leaders who are solving the world's greatest challenges. Guided by the belief that women are essential to progress in their communities, Vital Voices identifies and supports women with a daring vision for change. Through long-term investments that expand a woman's skills, connections, and visibility, Vital Voices accelerates and scales her impact. www.vitalvoices.org

- **Women's Democracy Network**
The International Republican Institute (IRI) and its sister organization, the National Democratic Institute for International Affairs, work to promote democracy globally. IRI established the Women's Democracy Network in 2006 to empower women around the world to participate in the political process and equip them with the skills needed to assume greater leadership roles in government, political parties, and civil society. www.iri.org, www.wdn.org

- **Women's Media Center (WMC)**
WMC is a progressive, nonpartisan, non-profit organization working to raise the visibility, viability, and decision-making power of women and girls in the media and ensure that their stories get told and their voices are heard. WMC does research, curates original content, educates women and girls on media savvy and interview skills, and maintains the SheSource database of more than 1,100 women experts on a wide array of topics. www.womensmediacenter.com

## Facts and Figures

- **Center for American Women in Politics (CAWP)**
CAWP, part of the Eagleton Institute of Politics at Rutgers, is nationally recognized as the leading source of scholarly research and current data about women's political participation in the U.S. Its mission is to promote greater knowledge and understanding about the role of women in U.S. politics, enhance women's influence in public life, and expand the diversity of women

in politics and government. www.cawp.rutgers.edu

- **Inter-Parliamentary Union (IPU)**
  The IPU has been collecting data on women in politics since the 1970s. Its databases list the number of women in national and regional parliaments, as well as the number of women cabinet ministers. It provides comparative data by country, as well as current world and regional averages. www.ipu.org

- **The U.S. Women, Peace and Security Index**[116]
  The Georgetown Institute for Women, Peace and Security has compiled this index, the first-ever ranking of women's rights and opportunities across 50 states and the District of Columbia, revealing the vast differences in the status of women across America. The index measures women's inclusion in the economy and politics as well as key aspects of justice and legal protections.

- ***The Women's Atlas***[117]
  Currently in its fifth edition, this book by Joni Seager provides a comprehensive and accessible analysis of global data on key issues such as equality, motherhood, women at work, women in the global economy, changing households, domestic violence, lesbian rights, women in government and politics, and more.

- **WomanStats Project**[118]
  WomanStats investigates the link between the security and behavior of states and the situation and security of women within those states. The project's database is the largest cross-national compilation of data, statistics, and maps on the status of women worldwide, with information on over 350 variables for 176 different countries.

- **World Economic Forum (WEF) Global Gender Gap Report**[119]
  Since 2006, the WEF Global Gender Gap Report has analyzed the laws and policies of 153 countries and benchmarked their progress against regional and global data that measure gender parity across four dimensions, including political participation. It also compares the relative status of and/or access to political opportunity for men and women.

These lists are available/updated at: stepheniefoster.com

# NOTES

1   Norris, Pippa, "The Impact of Electoral Reform on Women's Representation," ACTA Politica, 2006, available at https://bit.ly/3qkYwBV.

2   For an excellent summary, see Berger, Miriam, "2019 in Review: A Roller Coaster Ride for Women's Rights and Gender Equality Around the World," *The Washington Post*, December 26, 2109, https://wapo.st/2I21TME.

3   Hassan, Jennifer and O'Grady, Siobhán, "Female World Leaders Hailed as Voices of Reason Amid the Coronavirus Chaos," *The Washington Post*, April 20, 2020, https://wapo.st/2Jztq8G.

4   CAWP (Center for American Women and Politics) http://bit.ly/campRutgers.

5   "Record Number of Women to Serve in State Legislatures in 2021," Rutgers University Center for American Women and Politics, December 4, 2020, https://bit.ly/3neJo7j.

6   Nevada first reached this milestone following the 2018 elections, when 52.4% of its legislators were women. Fadel, Leila and Birkeland, Bente, "A First: Women Take the Majority in Nevada Legislature and Colorado House," NPR, February 4, 2019, https://n.pr/3qpSpwi.

7   Ibid.

8   Ibid.

9   Cosgrove, Jaclyn, "L.A. County Makes History with All Female Board of Supervisors," *Los Angeles Times*, November 4, 2020, https://lat.ms/39BZWCc.

10  The World Economic Forum, "The Global Gender Gap Report 2021," World Economic Forum, 2021, http://bit.ly/globalGenderGap.

11  Branigin, Anne, "The Pandemic Set Women's Equality Back Another Generation, a New Report Says," *The Lily*, March 31, 2021, http://bit.ly/theLilyWEF.

12  Peçanha, Sergio, "What Will It Take To Achieve Gender Equality in American Politics?" *The Washington Post*, August 21, 2020, https://wapo.st/36zbsMK.

13  Funk, Kendall D., "We Need Women's Leadership More Than Ever During Covid-19," The Gender Policy Report, University of Minnesota, May 5, 2020, https://bit.ly/39z9q0K. During the Trump Administration, the White House Coronavirus Task Force had only 9% women (2 of 22) and the Great American Economic Revival Industry Groups advising the White House on reopening the economy had less than 10% women (21 of 220).

14  Aspan, Maria, "Biden unveils COVID-19 task force that is 38% female and 69% underrepresented minority," November 9, 2020, https://bit.ly/3qnUIj5.

15  Council on Foreign Relations, "Women's Participation in Peace Processes," Council on Foreign Relations, updated January 30, 2019, https://on.cfr.org/37sp0st.

16  "Recommendations for Elevating the Role of Women in Mediation," The Institute for Inclusive Security, available at https://bit.ly/36wCfce, last visited August 20, 2020.

17  Dentzer, Bill and Lochhead, Colton, "Nevada Sees Many New Laws, But How Will They Affect You?" *Las Vegas Review-Journal*, June 10, 2019, https://bit.ly/3fXWpza.

18  Schwartz, Melissa, "Nevada Legislature Passes Final Step in Statewide Rape Kit Reform," Joyful Heart Foundation, June 24, 2019, https://bit.ly/2Vt8jYl.

19  Lochhead, Colton, "Nevada Legislature Liberalizes Abortion Rules," Las Vegas Review-Journal, May 21, 2019, https://bit.ly/3g3aRGg.

20  Kern, Leslie, "How to Rebuild Cities for Caregiving," Bloomberg, July 9, 2020 https://bloom.bg/3oiF076.

21  Spector, Dina, "Why Women Use Public Transit More Than Men," *Business Insider*, February 6, 2012, https://bit.ly/37sJ51U.

22  Ibid.

23  Ibid.

24  Foster, Stephenie, "Smart Cities Must Reflect Women's Transportation Needs," January 17, 2018, https://bit.ly/33DOFxk.

25  Pepera, Sandra, "Why Women in Politics?" Women Deliver, February 28, 2018, https://bit.ly/2VuJRG4.

26  Swiss, Liam, Fallon, Kathleen M., and Burgos, Giovani, "Does Critical Mass Matter? Women's Political Representation and Child Health in Developing Countries," *Social Forces*, 91(2), December 2012, 531-538, available at https://bit.ly/2I257Qg.

27  The study of countries belonging to the Organization of Economic Cooperation and Development (OECD) found that for every one percent increase in the number of women legislators, educational expenditures increased by 0.028 percentage points, a statistically significant amount. The research also found that having a more liberal or left-wing government per se did not impact educational expenditures and that the positive effect of women legislators does not depend on the country's parliamentary system. Chen, Li Ju, "Female Policymakers and Educational Expenditures: Cross Country Evidence," Research Papers in Economics, August 27, 2008 available at https://bit.ly/3g33m1H.

28  Norgaard, Kari and York, Richard, "Gender Equality and State Environmentalism," *Gender and Society*, 19(4), August 1, 2005 available at https://bit.ly/2L259ZG.

29  Bishin, Benjamin, and Cherif, Feryal M., "The Big Gains for Women's Rights in the Middle East, Explained," *The Washington Post*, July 23, 2018, https://wapo.st/2VufCiE.

30  Chattopadhyay, Raghabendra and Duflo, Esther, "Women as Policymakers: Evidence from a randomized policy experiment in India," *Econometrica*, 72(5), September 2004, available at https://bit.ly/2VAcPEh.

31  Bratton, Kathleen A. and Ray, Leonard P., "Descriptive Representation, Policy Outcomes & Municipal Day Care Coverage in Norway," *American Journal of Political Science*, 46(2), April 2002, available at https://bit.ly/33BkKpB.

32  Research summarized in Cammisa, Anne Marie and Reingold, Beth, "Women in State Legislatures and State Legislative Research: Beyond Sameness and Difference," *State Politics and Policy Quarterly*, 4(2), June 1, 2004, available at https://bit.ly/3ohtiKa. At the US federal level, however, women work on a wider range of issues.

33  Ibid.

34  Rosenthal, Cindy Simon, "Gender Styles in Legislative Committees," *Women and Politics*, 21(2), 2001, published online October 15, 2008, available at https://bit.ly/36uKsOm.

35  Morris, David Z., "These Representatives Want to Make Congress More Functional by Electing More Women–to Both Parties," *Fortune*, October 22, 2019, https://bit.ly/3oiGHS0.

36  "Politics: Women's Insight," Inter-Parliamentary Union, 2000, https://bit.ly/3qlCCye.

37  North, Anna, "America's Sexist Obsession with What Women Politicians Wear, Explained," Vox, December 3, 2018, https://bit.ly/2JEEJMY.

38  Henderson, Nia-Malika, "Barbara Mikulski Made It Okay for Women to Wear Pants in the Senate," *The Washington Post*, March 2, 2015, https://wapo.st/3qjRqgV.

39  Rogers, Kristen, "US Teens Use Screens More Than Seven Hours a Day on Average–and That's Not Including Schoolwork," CNN, October 19, 2019, https://cnn.it/37v3AuU.

40  Haraldsson, Amanda and Wängnerud, Lena, "The Effect of Media Sexism on Women's Political Ambition: Evidence from a Worldwide Study," *Feminist Media Studies*, 19(4), 2019, published online May 10, 2018, available at https://bit.ly/2VqxhaK.

41  Ibid.

42  Women's Media Center, "The Status of Women in the U.S. Media 2019," Women's Media Center, 2019, https://bit.ly/3lvEmRR.

43  Media Matters Staff, "Study: Women's Voices Marginalized in 2016 News Coverage of Foreign Affairs and National Security," Media Matters, March 8, 2017, https://bit.ly/3qlDFya.

44  Smith, Stacy L. & Cook, Crystal Allene, "Gender Stereotypes: An Analysis of Popular Films

and TV," Geena Davis Institute for Gender and the Media, 2008, https://bit.ly/33CTBlW.

45  Marcus, Jon, "The Degrees of Separation Between the Genders in College Keep Growing," *The Washington Post*, October 27, 2019, https://wapo.st/3ocy5w8.

46  New, Jake, "Getting Women to Run," Inside Higher Ed, November 4, 2014, https://bit.ly/3mAL8ap.

47  Ibid.

48  Pamela O'Leary and Shauna Shames, "Shattering the Glass Ceiling for Women in Politics," Scholars Strategy Network, November, 2013, https://bit.ly/3mC0N9t.

49  Nakamura, Reid, "How 'Will & Grace' Had a Real-Life Political Impact on Marriage Equality," The Wrap, September 28, 2017, https://bit.ly/3ly4A6j. As the article notes, "I think 'Will & Grace' probably did more to educate the American public than almost anything anybody has ever done so far," Vice President Joe Biden said on "Meet the Press" in 2012. "We knew when we were doing 'Will & Grace' that we were doing something important that was having social effect and political effect," star Debra Messing said in an interview shortly after Biden's comments in 2012.

50  Lewit, Meghan, "TV Drama Impacts Viewers' Health Behavior," USC News, September 19, 2007, https://bit.ly/3qjSVM5.

51  Papenfuss, Mary, "Geena Davis Tech Tool Totes Up Female Parity on Children's Programming," HuffPost, September 20, 2019, https://bit.ly/33ChLx0.

52  "Fact Sheet for the Fair Elections Program During the 2020 Election Cycle," Office of Campaign Finance, https://bit.ly/3lyufvV.

53  http://bit.ly/leadershipConnect

54  Burgat, Casey, "Among House Staff, Women are Well Represented. Just Not in the Senior Positions," *The Washington Post*, June 20, 2017, https://wapo.st/37v5k7q.

55  Foster, Stephenie and Markham, Susan, "Foreign Policy Congressional Committees Need to Call More Women Experts," *The Hill*, July 8, 2020, https://bit.ly/36zj2Hc.

56  Burgat, Casey, "Among House Staff, Women are Well Represented. Just Not in the Senior Positions," The Washington Post, June 20, 2017, https://wapo.st/37v5k7q.

57  For example, in the 2016 election, 55% of American women voted, while only 52% of men voted. In the 2018 midterm election, 53% of voters were women and 47% were men. "Gender Differences in Voter Turnout," Rutgers University Center for American Women in Politics, September 16, 2019, https://bit.ly/39BhluD. Further, there was a gender gap in turnout of young voters: 35.3% of women in that age group voted compared with 29.5% of men.

58  Ralph, Elizabeth, "The Women Who Don't Vote," Politico, February 21, 2020, https://politi.co/3lyv0oL.

59  Ibid.

60  Hamm, Nia, "MGH Doctor Starts Nationwide Patient Voter Registration Campaign," NBC Boston, July 31, 2020, https://bit.ly/2Vrh2Kr.

61  Staples, Brent, "When the Suffrage Movement Sold Out to White Supremacy," *The New York Times*, February 2, 2019, https://nyti.ms/3qjUdXr.

62  Ibid.

63  Weiss, Elaine, *The Women's Hour: The Great Fight to Win the Vote*, Penguin Random House, March 5, 2019.

64  "Democrat Rita Hart Abandons Election Challenge in House Race Decided by 6 Votes," NPR, http://bit.ly/6voteWin

65  Wood, Pamela, "Olszewski Affirmed as Winner of Democratic Primary for Baltimore County Executive," The Baltimore Sun, July 14, 2018, https://bit.ly/37x6Up4.

66  2019 Election Results, Virginia House of Delegates District 94, Virginia Public Access Project, https://bit.ly/3mtBo1E.

67  *The New York Times*, "New Mexico 29th District State House Results: David Adkins Leads," August 1, 2017, https://nyti.ms/39Fdg8H.

68  Salam, Maya, "The 6 Women Running for President Have Answers," *The New York Times*, June 21, 2019, https://nyti.ms/3og9Gpv.

69  Dittmar, Kelly, "What You Need to Know About the Record Numbers of Women Candidates in 2020," Center for American Women in Politics, August 10, 2020, https://bit.ly/2KVUxeF.

70  Ibid.

71  Ibid.

72  Miller, Claire Cain, "The Problem for Women is not Winning. It's Deciding to Run," *The New York Times*, October 25, 2016, https://nyti.ms/36ztj6d.

73  One arena in which women feel qualified, and are willing to run for office, is the local school board. A poll of school superintendents estimates that women represented 43% of the nation's school board members in the 2014-15 school year. Lawless, Jennifer L. and Fox, Richard L., "Men Rule: The Continued Under-representation of Women in US Politics," Women and Politics Institute, January 2012, https://bit.ly/39zgHxA.

74  Wasserman, Melanie, Gender Differences in Politician Persistence (November 27, 2018). Available at https://bit.ly/3g2klBn or https://bit.ly/3lAeDYF.

75  Lewis, Danny, "Victoria Woodhull Ran for President Before Women Had the Right to Vote," *Smithsonian Magazine*, May 10, 2016, https://bit.ly/39Fe8Kv.

76  "Victoria Woodhull," History of American Women Blog, https://bit.ly/3g3HtiM.

77  Wills, Matthew, "The Significance of Shirley Chisholm's Presidential Campaign," July 5, 2016, JSTOR Daily, https://bit.ly/33ETZk5.

78  "Hillary Clinton," Encyclopedia Britannica, available at http://bit.ly/hillaryClintonBio.

79  "Pelosi, Nancy," https://bit.ly/3g2luZH.

80  "Ferraro, Geraldine," https://bit.ly/2VsyUVB.

81  "Margaret Chase Smith: A Featured Biography," United States Senate, https://bit.ly/37p3fd4.

82  "Rankin, Jeanette," https://bit.ly/2KVVEel.

83  "Sarah Palin," Encyclopedia Britannica, https://bit.ly/39HhP2x.

84  "Mikulski, Barbara Ann," https://bit.ly/2I2fRy4.

85  "Kamala D. Harris,"https://bit.ly/37J5hFh.

86  "U.S. Supreme Court," Rutgers University Center for American Women in Politics, https://bit.ly/3lyzKe3.

87  Ibid.

88  Ibid.

89  Ibid.

90  Ibid.

91  Atske, Sara, et al., "The Share of Women in Legislatures Around the World is Growing, but They are Still Underrepresented," Pew Research Center, March 18, 2019, https://pewrsr.ch/39AfhD7.

92  "New IPU Report Shows Well-designed Quotas Lead to Significantly More Women MPs," Inter-Parliamentary Union, May 3, 2019, https://bit.ly/2JkhNCX.

93  Lijphart, Arend, *Patterns of Democracy: Government Forms and Performance in Thirty-Six Countries*, Yale University Press, Second Edition 2012, available at https://bit.ly/3ofIgQK.

94  Norris, Pippa, "The Impact of Electoral Reform on Women's Representation," ACTA Politica, 2006, available at https://bit.ly/3qkYwBV.

95  Office of the Clerk, "New Zealand Women MPs Continuing to Break Barriers," New Zealand Parliament, March 8, 2019, https://bit.ly/37sQD4P.

96  O'Niell, Aaron, "Number of Countries with Women in Highest Position of Executive Power 1960 - 2020," Statista, August 4, 2020, https://bit.ly/36xxDTx.

97  UN Women, "Facts and Figures: Leadership and political participation," UN Women, available at https://bit.ly/3lyAW11 updated April 2021.

98  http://bit.ly/womenGovLeaders.

99    Globally, the number of women holding local government offices is unknown. Currently, there is no global baseline to track the proportion of women represented in local government, constituting a major knowledge gap. In the U.S., Since 1971, the number of women serving in state legislatures has more than quintupled. "Women in Elected Office 2018," Center for American Women in Politics, https://bit.ly/3lycHjh.

100   Inter-Parliamentary Union, "Women in Politics: 2020." March 2021, https://www.ipu.org/resources/publications/infographics/2020-03/women-in-politics-2020

101   Atske, Sara et al., "The Share of Women in Legislatures Around the World is Growing, But They Are Still Underrepresented," Pew Research Center, March 18, 2019, https://pewrsr.ch/39AfhD7.

102   Inter-Parliamentary Union. "Women in National Parliaments," as of February 1, 2019 updated at https://bit.ly/39A8Y2l as of August 20, 2020.

103   Powley, Elizabeth, "Rwanda: The Impact of Women Legislators on Policy Outcomes Affecting Children and Families," UNICEF, December 2006, https://uni.cf/37sh8ay.

104   Hughes, Melanie M. and Tripp, Aili Mari, "Civil War and Trajectories of Change in Women's Political Representation in Africa, 1985–2010" *Social Forces* 93(4) 1513-1540, June 2015, available at https://bit.ly/36uAKeP.

105   Smith, Stacy L. and Cook, Crystal Allene, "Gender Stereotypes: An Analysis of Popular Films and TV," Geena Davis Institute for Gender and the Media, 2008, https://bit.ly/33CTBlW.

106   Women's Media Center, "The Status of Women in the U.S. Media 2019," Women's Media Center, 2019, https://bit.ly/3lvEmRR.

107   Moskvitch, Katia, "The BBC has a Pay Gap; Here's How to Fix It," *Wired*, October 24, 2018, https://bit.ly/3qpjqQb. Further, as a result, the BBC was formally investigated and after a yearlong review, the U.K. Equality and Human Rights Commission concluded there was reason to suspect that "some women at the organisation have not received equal pay for equal work." The resulting scandal prompted several high-profile employees such as Jeremy Vine and John Humphrys to take substantial pay cuts, with some choosing to leave the BBC altogether.

108   Anna Bressanin, personal Interview, March 18, 2019, cited in DiMeco, Lucina, "#ShePersisted: Women, Politics & Power in the New Media World," The Wilson Center, Fall 2019, available at https://bit.ly/3lyis0u.

109   Robehmed, Natalie, "Jennifer Lawrence Speaks Out on Making Less Than Male Co-Stars," *Forbes*, October 13, 2015, https://bit.ly/3g2xBG8.

110   Elkins, Kathleen, "Michelle Williams Getting 1 Percent of Mark Wahlberg's Fee is Not Actually that Unusual for Hollywood," CNBC, January 11, 2018, https://cnb.cx/39zkF9s.

111   Chmielewski, Dawn, "Yes, Mark Wahlberg's $1.5 Million Check To The Time's Up Legal Defense Fund Cleared," Deadline, March 11, 2018, https://deadline.com/2018/03/mark-wahlberg-times-up-sxsw-wage-disparity-melinda-gates-1202335459/

112   Masullo, Gina M., et al., "Women Journalists and Online Harassment, The University of Texas at Austin Center for Media Engagement, April 2018, https://bit.ly/2L2OepR.

113   Women's Media Center, "The Status of Women in the U.S. Media 2019," Women's Media Center, 2019, p. 29. https://bit.ly/3lvEmRR.

114   Grieco, Elizabeth, "Newsroom Employees are Less Diverse than U.S. Workers Overall," Pew Research Center, November 2, 2018, https://pewrsr.ch/39Aljne.

115   York, Catherine, "Women Dominate Journalism Schools, but Newsrooms are Still a Different Story," Poynter, September 18, 2017, https://bit.ly/39BrtUg.

116   https://giwps.georgetown.edu/usa-index/

117   Seager, Joni, *The Women's Atlas*, Penguin Random House, October 30, 2018, available at https://bit.ly/37FmD5V.

118   www.womanstats.org

119   www.weforum.org

# Index

# Appendix

## A Framework for Advocacy & Action

**1.**
Identify an issue you care about.

**2.**
Research: Do current laws or programs disadvantage women
and/or girls?

**3.**
Investigate the context in order to understand the landscape.

**4.**
Learn who has the power to make changes.

**5.**
Define your interest in this issue.

**6.**
Prepare your questions.

**7.**
Develop suggestions for solving the challenges you are raising.

**8.**
Ask your questions and outline your suggestions.

**9.**
What's next? Follow up!

## Take Action in Your Daily Life!

Made in the USA
Middletown, DE
23 July 2022

69763427R00097